"Because you are alive, everything is possible."

Thich Nhat Hanh

ISBN: 9781097564309

Cover design by Iro Ouranou

SHINE MANIFESTO

Find Your Authentic Self,
Live Your Authentic Life.

Chris Brock

For Victoria and Luna Poppy

I write, erase, rewrite,
Erase again, and then
A poppy blooms.

— Hokushi (1667–1718)

Table of Contents

Introduction

***"The days are long, but the years are short." –
Gretchen Rubin***

If you were to try and count all the stars in the night's
sky, all the stars in the universe, you could count one
every second for seventy years and never even scratch
the surface. There are more stars in the universe than
there are grains of sand on all the world's beaches. Each
of those stars is a sun just like ours – some of them a bit
smaller, some of them a million times larger – and all
burning fearsomely hot and blindingly bright.

At the heart of each of these suns are nuclear processes
of heat and pressure that transfer energy from one
form to another. Atoms are split and fused,
transformed into other elements. Shapes shift, states
change, and in all its new forms energy is jettisoned, hot
and alive, into the ether.

From these furnaces of creation energy is propelled in
all directions, as gravity waves that distort time and
space, as chemical compounds that clump together to
become planets of rock and water, and as gas and dust
that become incomprehensibly vast clouds of myriad
colours that illuminate the cosmos like rainbows a
billion miles long.

This dance of energy and matter makes up everything
we know, and since time began this transference from
star to matter to particle to wave to photon and
electron, backwards and forwards, never destroyed but

only transferred, has given birth to everything we know, and everything we don't know.

The atoms that in our bodies, and the fuel that keeps them running, were born in the middle of suns just like our own. We are, quite literally, made of stardust.

This energy makes up all of existence. From the rusty nail that we tore our trousers on when we were children climbing over fences, to the clouds we imagined into different shapes as we lay in the summer grass with our teenage crushes, to the diamond we slip onto the finger of our beloved as adults, and our favourite comfy chair by the window that we sit on as we enjoy our golden years.

This energy makes up everything, from the things that we can touch and feel, to the breeze on our face, the thoughts in our minds, and the blood that pumps through the veins of our bodies. It is life itself, and with every action energy is transferred into a different state, and different place. The sun gives up its energy to the farthest reaches of the cosmos, and we feel its warmth on our face on a summer evening. The drummer gives up his energy and it is transformed into the rhythm that ignites enthusiasm of the crowd. The logs give up their energy to warm a house and turn to ash in the process, the cup of tea grows cold on the windowsill.

Just as energy only remains in one form fleetingly, so too is our life on this earth a fleeting dalliance that is all consuming while it occurs, and then it's on to the next thing. We are energy, we are of it, from it, and just like it our life will be transferred to the next thing faster than you know. Blink and you'll miss it.

And while our brief moments of conscious existence in this life may seem insignificant in the grand scheme of things – after all, this planet quickly shrinks to nothingness against the near infinite scale of the universe – it provides us with a unique opportunity. An opportunity to explore, to play and to create. To experience life and the notion of being.

We have been placed in a sandpit bigger than our human minds can comprehend. And here we can engage with beauty, experiment with the limitless capabilities of our imaginations, be anything we want to be, do anything we want to do, and go anywhere we want to go. We can spend our energy singing, dancing, painting, playing, and laughing. We can recreate ourselves as gods one day, and animals the next. We are boundless, shapeless, unique and omnipotent. We are limited only by the borders of our imagination.

Yet we have shrunk our world. We have built walls, systems, processes and categories that we try to fit ourselves into, that we structure our lives around, that we give much more importance to that we really should. In our effort to get by and to quantify where we are, we have constructed imaginary limits that keep us caged like ornamental budgerigars when our nature is to fly unlimited on the breeze.

Yet within this cage we have lost this beautiful truth behind countless human constructs that restrict us, divide us, fill up our capacity for imagination, and prevent us from flying. We create fictions about ourselves and those around us, which serve to hold us back, to keep us apart from our brothers and sisters, and to stop us realising our uninhibited potentiae for wonderful things.

In the context of a million galaxies, do you think it matters what people think of your new shoes? In the context of a billion suns, is it really conceivable that national borders represent anything other than a child-race attempting to divide itself? In the context of infinite space and time do you think that all those things that make you angry really count for anything?

We spend so much energy tearing ourselves and each other down, when that same energy could be built building ourselves up. We waste so much emotional energy on envy and anger and bitterness and fear, when it could be spent on love, on joy, on happiness and laughter. We put all our effort into scorching the earth, when we could be reaching to the moon.

We have been given an infinite canvas to paint upon, and yet we find ourselves wrapped up in minutiae that serve no purpose other than to shrink our perspective, narrow our dreams, and prevent us from exploring everything that life has to offer. Everything that we have to offer.

We are so busy reading the latest political scandal in the newspaper, as we run for the bus, worried that we'll be late for work again, that we fail to notice the sound of the breeze blowing through the trees. We are so consumed with our likes and retweets that we fail to smell the freshly baked bread as we pass the café on the corner. We are so stressed by simply getting by, from one day to the next, that we fail to notice the wings on our backs.

Deep down in all of us there is a poetry and a rhythm that wants to be set free. Behind the clothes we wear to the office, and the tribe that we associate ourselves with is a unique, formless being who could revel in joy, if we could only break out of the chrysalis that keeps our true butterfly nature trapped. For all of us there is an authentic life that promises us more riches than we could imagine, if only we could learn to let go of stigma, of dogma, of our history, our traumas, our biases, our pride and our ego.

Hiding in plain sight, both in front of and behind our eyes, there is everything we could possibly want, everything we could possibly imagine, everything that both is and isn't. There is boundless joy and infinite love, the chance to fulfil our potential and truly be. Vast oceans of possibility stretch out before us, and all we need to do is dip in a toe and test the water.

We hang so much of our lives on that which we can count and measure, we associate so much of our identities with that which we have, that which has gone before, or that which is expected of us, that we fail to ever see beyond the superficial and the tangible. We are unable to see who we truly are and live the infinite, authentic lives that we truly deserve, because we have attached so much of ourselves to things that aren't us, but which give us something to cling to.

We become our insecurities. We become the victims of unfortunate circumstances. We become products of the past. We become the childhood nickname that the bullies called us. We become 'person most likely to...' and we cling to these things, because it's easier to be the mask that we hide behind than it is to remove it and see who we truly are.

We are frightened to step into the darkness and meet ourselves, because finding our power and our potential means facing our weaknesses and our limitations. Because finding our true, naked, authentic selves means taking responsibility for it. And we're not sure we're strong enough for that.

But we are.

And when we finally summon up the courage to step into the darkness and switch on the light, we will find ourselves emancipated, liberated and rejuvenated. We will find ourselves transported to a new world where the things we took for granted take on a new significance, where the things that seemed so important to us now seem like mere trifles, and everywhere we turn flowers blossom, birds sing, the sun shines, and music plays. Suddenly we have found life, and it has found us.

When we are no longer controlled by the anger that keeps us apart from others, we are free to reach out to them, to help them and heal them, and to let them help us. When we are no longer controlled by fear, we are free to experience joy, to create art and to build for ourselves the lives we always dreamed about. When we are no longer restricted by what we can buy, touch and feel, we are free to explore the infinite possibilities of our imaginations, of the real world here on the surface, and the abstract worlds that lie beneath.

We can release ourselves from the world of what can be measured and quantified and explore new landscapes of comprehension, of being, and of love. And as our love for the world around us and the people we share it with grows, we can learn to love ourselves too. We can realise that we aren't the anxieties and negative thought patterns that dominate our waking and sleeping minds. We aren't the sum of our past experiences. We aren't the worst versions of ourselves that we see when we look in the mirror, but we are free to be reborn, free to forgive ourselves, free to love ourselves and appreciate ourselves. Free to find out who we really are.

And when we who we want to be, not who we believe we are supposed to be based on external influences, the world around us will begin to change. Now, without the need for anyone's permission or validation, we will find ourselves empowered and surrounded by beauty.

We will be able to shrink ourselves until we can look up at the flowers that tower above us, offering us shade from the glorious sunshine. We will be able to grow until we can hide the moon under our thumb and play marbles with the planets. We will be able to explore entire universes that don't even exist yet, and travel backwards and forwards in time to chat with Shakespeare and shake hands with our great, great, great grandchildren.

When we free ourselves from the shackles of our own inner dialogue and empower ourselves to live our lives instead of the lives of others, we will see beauty and riches, both real and metaphorical, in all directions. Cloudy days will bring joy, raindrops will appear as disco balls inviting us to dance through puddles, and the crayon drawings of a three-year-old will hold more magic than the Mona Lisa.

When we open our minds to the possibility of beauty, we will see it everywhere. When we open ourselves to the possibility of our own strength and power, it will course through our veins. And when we let go of our pain and allow life to find us, we will be immersed in it, cradled and supported in its effervescent light.

Time is passing for us in this life. It will continue to pass whatever we do. It will pass if we focus on our anger and hurt, and it will pass if we surround ourselves with love. It will pass if we busy ourselves making excuses to hide from life, and it will pass if we busy ourselves in the garden watching the bees dance from flower to flower. Today there are 24 hours, and some days seem like an eternity. But decades can pass between breaths, and we wonder where they went.

Better to spend those years making art instead of excuses, sharing love instead of hatefulness, being extraordinary instead of ordinary, and deciding what we will do with this wonderful opportunity called life. How will we spend our energy? How will we light up this tiny, beautiful corner of our universe?

The peony bud,
When opening,
Shoots forth a rainbow.

— Yosa Buson

PROLOGUE

When Dame Gillian Lynne was only seven years old, she had nearly driven her mother to the end of her tether.

The little girl could not sit still and was underperforming at school. She was constantly fidgeting, leaping around, disrupting class and refusing to focus on what the teacher – or anyone else for that matter – was saying. It was suspected she was hyperactive or had a learning disorder because she would just not conform. So her mother took her to see a doctor.

The doctor listened intently to their story, and then asked the little girl if he could speak to her mother in private. As the two adults left the room, the doctor switched on the radio, and from outside they observed through the window as the little girl danced around his office. He turned to her mother and said:

"She doesn't have a disorder, she's a born dancer."

In the years to come she would graduate from the Royal Ballet and be awarded the title of Dame Commander of the Order of the British Empire for Services to dance and musical theatre.

What a strange thing!
to be alive
beneath cherry blossoms.

— Kobayashi Issa

Chapter 1
A System of Dissatisfaction

"It is no measure of health to be well adjusted to a profoundly sick society." – **Jiddu Krishnamurti**

If you're reading this, chances are you're subject to a system that promised you the world but has so far failed to deliver. A system that 99% of us have bought into, for one reason or another, and yet we have never managed to take advantage of all that it has to offer. The potential for abundance, the potential for happiness, the potential for completeness.

We are brought up to believe that if we do everything by the book, follow the rules and work our way up the ladder in an orderly manner, we will find riches and prosperity. All our material, spiritual, emotional and mental wants and needs will be met by a system that has our best interests at heart. The system, we are told, has been designed and built over hundreds of generations to deliver everything we could ever want, so long as we work hard enough and follow the rules.

We are fed the story, from a very early age, that if we educate ourselves, give our all to our employers and doff our caps to the powers that be, then we will have a happy, comfortable life. And if we don't have a happy, comfortable life, then it is a sign that we – and not the system – are broken. We're not clever enough, smart enough, worthy enough.

We are not good enough.

Only, this system, this western capitalist system, has us entranced by an illusion. We are led to believe a lie, instructed to follow rules that should lead us to everything we've worked so hard for our entire lives – our just rewards – but in truth the whole thing is a myth. We believed that if we worked hard, did everything that we were supposed to do, we would find happiness and contentment. And while the system would have us believe that this is the natural order of things, the reality is actually the opposite.

The reason the system needs us to believe these fallacies is because it isn't working for our benefit, despite what we may think. It is not for us. Instead the system is fuelled by us and, in particular, our dissatisfaction. It relies on us being unhappy with ourselves, with our situation, with our material wealth, and most of all, it relies on us lacking in self-esteem and confidence.

If we were all to find contentment, the current system would fail completely. If we were to find happiness, it would all come grinding to a halt. If we were to wake up to the realisation that we already have everything we need – both materially and spiritually – and that we no longer need to keep buying stuff, the whole machine would break down. The wheels would fall off.

That's because the commercial system that we've been born into, that ascribes a monetary value to our education, to our politics, whose products we buy and whose debt we accrue, requires us to be constantly wanting. It requires that we are always hungry, in a state of lack, needing more, being unhappy with where we are, what we've got and who we are. It needs us to feel incomplete, because it can only function if we believe that it can complete us. Which, most of the time, it cannot.

It needs us to believe that we won't be beautiful unless we have the latest skin care treatment or hair dye. That we won't get a proper shave unless we have the latest razor system or aftershave balm. We won't have any friends, or any kind of happy life, unless we squeeze ourselves into the new fashions, the new cars, the new trends, the new stuff that exists purely to extract our money and our self-esteem from us. The stuff that exists purely to milk us in order that the wheels keep on turning.

And to do this, it feeds us impossible notions of perfection and utopia.

Those people we see in the commercials, cavorting on the beaches in their skin-tight jeans, smiles plastered across their faces, as they drink the newest diet beverage – they're not real people. They're representations of something that doesn't exist. A false reality that we all aspire to, but which is essentially unattainable. These people are fictional characters played by actors and models who hadn't actually met until that morning, and when they're not portraying perfection they're struggling with the realities of cooking, cleaning and doing the laundry just like the rest of us.

The system that we find ourselves in is promising the impossible, because it needs us to be forever wanting more, better, bigger. It needs us to crave the latest smartphone, even though our current one works perfectly well. It needs us to be dissatisfied with ourselves so that we'll buy into the latest fad, the latest diet, or the latest thing that would make us better people if only we had enough space left on our credit cards to buy it. It needs us to keep chasing after the carrot that dangles inches from the end of our nose just out of reach, and we're blinded to the fact that all we're getting is the stick.

And the whole thing keeps chugging along.

This system only serves itself. We are fuel for its engine, grist for its mill, and while we think this whole thing is all about us – perhaps even for us – the truth of the matter is we work only to keep its cogs turning. We earn enough so that we can buy what we need and pay our taxes. We get only enough sleep that we can just about function in the job that pays us. We sleepwalk through a daily routine that exists just to keep us going through our daily routine, with access to just enough money that we can pay for the things that keep the system alive, its pockets lined, and its mechanism greased, but little more.

We are numbers in a giant number crunching machine. It is a machine that doesn't see or appreciate us as individuals, with imaginations, personalities, desires and values, but a machine that works more efficiently if we can fit into the pigeon holes that it creates for us. It needs to categorise us, fit us into cliques, tribes, age brackets, racial groups, and risk profiles. We are sorted, processed, managed, categorised, funnelled, and profiled.

It prevents us from breaking free from its allure by feeding us things to keep ourselves distracted. New forms of entertainment to occupy our minds, new things to be afraid of, new gossip to share, new groups of people to hate or be outraged by. Trifles and trivialities that fill up our capacity, so we don't think for ourselves and challenge the status quo.

And what's more, by denying our own unique human attributes and buying into the manufactured communities and tribes of the system, we do the system's work for it. We sort, process, manage, categorise, funnel and profile ourselves. We change ourselves so that we can fit into the categories – the pigeon holes – that the system finds easiest to quantify, process and use. We turn ourselves into measurable quantities rather than magical entities.

Whole industries are built around the idea that people like us, who do things like that, can be treated like this. Algorithms know what kind of products to advertise to us. Computer programs which know what we did last can predict what we'll do next. We are the fodder for trillion-dollar industries, faceless nuggets of data rich in dollar-value, but lacking in human uniqueness. You looked at this, so you'll most likely want to buy this. You spoke to this person and travelled to this location, so you might be a threat to the system. You are not interested in algebra, so your career choices will be limited, and you'll be labelled a trouble maker.

Are you a threat?

You are a girl so you will wear pink, you are a boy so you will wear blue. You have a place and you should know it. It's not for you to question authority. It's not for you to step out of your box. It's not for you to challenge, or to wonder why, or to do anything other than what's expected, what's intended, and what works for the system. It's not for you to disobey your programming. Get to work at nine, go home at five. Monday to Friday. With two days off.

That's the format. The nature of things. Fit in or be cast out.

Do not, under any circumstances, think for yourself. Just think what we feed you, consume what we sell you, do what we tell you, be who we want you to be.

Never, ever, colour outside the lines.

We are consumers. Cattle who feed at the trough of daytime television while we are milked of anything that can keep the system limping along. We are juiced daily; our energy and enthusiasm extracted to oil the wheels and keep the cogs turning. We are the coke that fuels the aged turbines of the ancient steam engine, a sick old machine that values money more than kindness, power more than compassion, and division more than unity.

Times, though, are changing.

While most of us are blinkered, condemned to the treadmill of the daily routine, blinded by the daily two-minute hate that makes us feel like we stand for something and we're making a difference – the outrage on twitter, the pre-digested non-think of the news media, anything that makes us feel like we are activists, protesting the pantomime baddies who are paraded before us – some of us are starting to see the system for the hamster wheel of distraction that it is. And many are saying "this is not for me".

As history repeats itself and nothing ever seems to change, as the pendulum swings from one side to the other, and then back again as surely as the sun follows the moon and the day follows the night, we're starting to look for new ways to navigate our journey from beginning to end other than along those paths laid out for us like train tracks by those who have gone before. We are starting to find our power, and the strength to choose for ourselves which direction to go in, which rules to follow, which to break, and how best to make choices that serve us, instead of the system.

We are coming off the rails, and maybe – just maybe – we like the way it feels.

Can we exist in the system without being subject to it? Can we make it work for us? Can we turn our relationship with the leaking battleship of western civilisation into a dance, a game, a reality that serves us, rather than the other way around?

Can we choose to disengage from the cattle trough that we're offered and opt to graze from lush, green pastures instead? Is there another way of living? A way that will give us everything that we have ever wanted, that will deliver on the promises that the western system has failed to deliver, and which will allow us to live a life of contentment, happiness and satisfaction?

We have been so blinkered by the default reality of this shallow surface world – so conditioned to fit in – that we have become oblivious to the answers that are right in front of us. We have become such products of the system that we have forgotten our humanity. Yet it is this humanity that will enable us to step aside and realise a different version of reality that we can create for ourselves.

For generations we have been trying to fit in with the rigid framework of a broken society when we ourselves are not rigid. We have been told to fear anyone who doesn't fit in with the predetermined notion of what normal people are like, when this notion of normality isn't natural at all.

We are unique, unusual, strange and beautiful – immaculately amorphous – but we are required to conform, fit in, dress the same, think the same, be the same, suppress our intrinsic dynamism. The system needs us to be uniform, regimented and ordered in order that it can quantify us, and to achieve this we have been duped out of our natural tendencies of being interesting, different, and human. The child who spins around, singing with his arms outstretched is medicated because he's deemed to be abnormal and hyperactive. But the reality is that he is the normal one, he is the one embracing his unique humanity, while the rest of us have been hammered into shape, to fit perfectly into neatly arranged cubicles, where we can sit in front of screens and process data. Row after row, like battery hens laying eggs for our masters.

When was the last time you stretched out your arms and wiggled your fingers? When was the last time you screamed out with glee? When was the last time you were undeniably human?

There is a light that shines within all of us. A glowing ball of energy. But it has become buried by paperwork, routines, rules, regulations, boiling the kettle, crossing the road, contracts, uniforms, appropriate attire, printer drivers, rent payments, sim cards, orderly queues and sensible shoes. It is lost beneath this season's fashions, TV listings, bus timetables, political scandals, insurance renewals and firmware updates.

As we trudge through life, adopting the false constructs of Monday to Friday, nine-to-five, paycheque to paycheque, we are blind to the straitjackets that keep us from spreading our wings. We find ourselves thinking that it's bonkers to hug a tree or make snow angels or daisy chains, when it's surely bonkers not to. We think it's peculiar and weird when someone sings in the street, but as we're all equipped with singing voices isn't it peculiar and weird that we don't? We think the people dancing around the lamppost at midday on a Tuesday must be mad or drunk, but with arms and legs and the ability to comprehend joy, surely, it's madness that we are not.

We aren't machines, but we behave as if we are. We are humans, but we medicate those who behave like it. Anyone who colours outside the lines must be brought back inside. Anyone who realises their true nature and decides to make life work for them, must be put to work at the coal face for their own sake – but really, it's for the sake of the system.

It's the system that's bizarre and our conformity and uniformity that's insane. We are encouraged to hate each other, to compete against each other, and to obsess on imaginary notions of boundaries and borders, abstract concepts of money and status, and to fixate on the differences that once made us interesting, but now make us enemies.

And all of this to keep a broken system and its broken leaders ticking along.

But we don't need to go off grid to make life work for us. We don't need to move to a commune or become billionaires or adopt eccentric new personas – although you are more than welcome to if you wish. All you have to do is something that connects you with your humanity. Do something that reflects your uniqueness. Do something extra.

We must do something, anything, that is our own, that belongs to us and is not defined – or instructed – by the system. Anything at all. Just do something. Create something. Build something. Something more. Something beyond the day-to-day. Plant the seeds of our own identities, our own humanity, and let them grow. Let them flourish. Forget about the fears and the anxieties that this system needs us to embrace in order to stay dissatisfied, and find the things that interest us, that nourish our souls, and use these things to take our lives from the ordinary to the extraordinary.

We can be in the system, but we must not be of the system.

Millions of people are doing this already. They're all around us, among us, living just like regular human beings. Except they are engaged with life on a different level, in a different way, that takes their existence from the ordinary, the usual and the conventional, to one of a life well lived – a life of satisfaction and contentment. You probably brushed past one of these strange and exceptional characters on the street on your way to work. One of them might share your office. Another might stand next to you in the lunch queue. Another might be sat in the plane that flies overhead when you're busy looking down into your smartphone. One of them might order more stationary when the office runs out of pens.

It could be your lazy colleague who runs marathons at the weekend. It might be the boring girl in accounts who goes to conventions dressed as a cartoon character. It might be the guy at the next desk who has transformed his loft into a miniature railway and plays station master into the small hours of the morning. It might be the austere woman who answers the phone, but gives up her spare time to help those less able than herself feed themselves or dress themselves. It could be the junior manager who engages in angry protest marches against the capitalist elite every weekend, smashing the windows of chain stores and daubing political slogan across government buildings.

It could be the office temp with the unique idea that will become a billion-dollar business in five years' time, or the teenager hanging around the bus stop with a radical idea for a new type of political system.

All of these people are finding purpose outside of the confines of the system. All of these people finding ways to be extra, to embrace their unique non-conformity, and relish their uniqueness. They are souls with a body, not the other way around. They are finding ways to live beyond their job title and their salary band. They are colouring outside the lines, because they know that inside the lines everything is black and white and mundane and uninteresting. They find their freedom in ways that allow them to do and be more.

They're not just here to make up the numbers. They're here to live.

All it requires is an extra sense of purpose in order to break the death grip of the system. For some that means a hobby that gives them a sense of purpose. For others it means spending their spare time helping people, sharing and giving. For others it means starting multi-million-dollar businesses that span the globe and change the world. But behind it all is a desire to do more, to be more, to extract more meaning out of life, and own it for themselves. Creating a little corner of reality that no-one else can take away or have influence over. It can be something as small as an allotment growing vegetables, or as huge as a new global social initiative.

You are already unique, special and extraordinary. You are already made of atoms that were born in the hearts of stars. How long will you wait before you do your thing? Your wonderful, magical thing?

Behold the white wisterias —
The Milky Way blown by the wind.

—   Hayano Hajin

Chapter 2
The Mirage of Petty Rewards

"It is difficult to free fools from the chains they revere."
– Voltaire

On the dusty high plain, the wind blows sharply and the sand cuts through air. The trees – what few there are – grow sideways, and it seems cold, barren and unfit for anything that would wish to live here. Somewhere, though, there is life. In the distance it is just possible to hear the sound of cattle and sheep, the dull tone of cowbells just audible, carried along on the wind.

A robed man appears in the distance, covered from head to toe to protect him from the dust and sand. As he gets closer the bird on his arm comes into view, its cowl shielding it from the harsh conditions as it rests, waiting to be awoken. Waiting to go to work.

The robed man comes to a place that is as good as any, removes the hood from his bird and rouses it. The falcon opens its eyes slowly, blinded for a moment by the bright sunlight that beats down on this arid land. Stretching, it shakes its perfectly preened wings and feels the air, blinking in the dusty wind. It pauses for a moment and then its master sets his bird flying, calling out as it climbs into the sky, scanning the world below in search of prey.

Perhaps today it will catch a skylark or a sparrow, maybe grouse, a duck or a rabbit. The keen eye of the falcon searches for the tell-tale movements that betray its target. At these heights few of the creatures it is hunting are even aware of the bird's presence, but with its highly-evolved visual acuity it misses very little, apart from the obvious truths that are right in front of it. This bird has been trained to deny its innate purpose, yet it feels grateful for the enforced servitude that it has no idea it has been lured into.

Now it sees something and suddenly it swoops, wings back, torpedo-like until, with talons outstretched, it catches its prey. A moment of wrestling and victory is won. The bird stands on its catch, gripped tight in its claw as it surveys the landscape. The world is desolate, beautiful and unforgiving, yet teeming with the abundant life that is all around if you have the eyes to see it. The falcon lived out here once, but it doesn't remember.

Each time the falcon returns to the gloved hand of its master with its fare in its claws, the master wraps the bird's leather leash around his little finger, or puts it under his thumb, to prevent the falcon taking flight again. And the hunter rewards his bird with a tasty morsel in exchange for the spoils of its battle.

The bird is in the employ of its master, the falconer, and does his bidding. It goes out to hunt, focused on the search for prey, and in return it is well cared for. It is kept clean and warm, fed and watered, and it understands that this comfortable life will always continue as long as it returns to the gloved hand each time and hands over its prey.

But the bird is always hungry.

The falconer knows the value of a hungry bird. A hungry bird will always hunt, because it desires the reward. But the reward is never enough to satisfy its hunger, as a bird that is sated will not serve its master. A bird that is well fed – 'fed up' – no longer has any incentive to hunt. It will instead find a perch to sit and digest its food, unwilling to return to the falconer's hand until it is hungry again. A bird that is fed up leaves its master hungry, and the master cannot hunt for his own dinner.

When the hunt is over, the leash is wrapped around the little finger or placed under the thumb and the bird is blindfolded with a hood. In the 16th Century this was called hoodwinking, to prevent the bird from being distracted until it was required to hunt again, or until it was safely in its cage. A hoodwinked bird is a calm bird. A hungry bird is a useful bird.

From inside its hood the falcon doesn't see the other birds, flying free, arching and swooping in the sky, calling to each other, eating their own prey rather than returning it to a master who keeps them warm and watered and caged and under the thumb. From inside its hood the falcon just considers the next hunt and the reward it will receive after its hard work is done. From inside its hood it does, perhaps, dream of flying free, but it knows that this can only ever be a dream. Ignorance is bliss.

When it's on the wing, the falcon is so focused on doing its job that it doesn't notice the other birds resting in the trees, their stomachs full of meals captured on an abundant plain overflowing with food. When it's on the wing the falcon is just focused on doing the thing that will lead to its tasty treat.

When it is on the wing, or wearing the hood, the falcon doesn't realise that it can feast like a king outside the employment of the falconer. It doesn't realise that while it works for its master it is destined to a life of constant hunger, of constant servitude. But if it were to just fly off in search of its own destiny it will never go hungry again, and will find a life of abundant reward.

It doesn't realise these things because the falconer controls what it thinks and sees. The falconer keeps the bird from seeing what's beyond the hood, or beyond the hunt. The falconer needs the bird more than the bird needs him, but it is vital that the bird is kept in this state of illusion in order that the falconer can exist at all. If the bird was to fly away for a life of its own, the falconer would starve to death. If all the birds were to leave their falconers, they would all be free to enjoy the abundance of a world that is right in front of them, but which they are yet to experience because their view of the world is controlled by their master.

The birds are controlled and manipulated because they are always in a state of hunger. The birds will remain trapped as long as they are wanting more. But like the other birds they could be free if they could just accept that already have enough. They have the skills and the ability to feed themselves a hundred times over if they decided to. Yet each time they return their catch and receive a tiny tasty morsel as reward. This reward is guaranteed, and that is reassuring and safe.

The robed man needs the status quo to remain. The bird is petted, groomed, watered and housed. And it is trained and manipulated. It receives petty rewards when it does as the master wishes, and it is punished when it doesn't. It is made to feel like royalty with a shining bell around its neck, so it can be found should it ever wander too far. And in return the bird feeds its master by returning with its prey. And with enough meat left to sell at the market, the falconer has become rich, his robes flowing and adorned with gold thread, his large house filled with art and luxuries. The falconer's success is built upon the back of the bird.

Yet the bird will always be hungry, and the bell will always be a symbol of its captivity unless it decides, one day, to keep its catch for itself. And when that day comes it will realise that it no longer needs its master, and that its master was its jailor. And as it flies higher and higher, above the now lush and abundant grassland, growing grateful and content with a belly full of the spoils of its own hunt, somewhere behind it, a long way away on the horizon where the land is dusty and dry, its former master cries desperately for its return. Powerless, hungry, he will have to feed himself now.

If he only knew how.

The crow has flown away:
Swaying in the evening sun,
A leafless tree.

— Natsume Soseki

Chapter 3
The Paradox of Wanting

"It is quite impossible to unite happiness with a yearning for what we don't have." – Epictetus

The world is a kaleidoscope. With every twist and turn it opens itself up to myriad different interpretations, shining new shapes and colours in all directions, revealing something for everyone, if they know how to look at it.

It is both light and dark, hot and cold, and offers a limitless variety of experiences for us to indulge ourselves in. A cornucopia of choices to be made and lived. Every choice we make sends us in a different direction, and every day we make choices that influence our path through life. What we do today will impact where we find ourselves in decades to come.

Most of the time, we don't realise that the world we are experiencing and the life we are living are the result of the choices we have made in the past. Most of the time we don't realise we are making choices at all. Instead we feel that we are subjects of luck — most of it bad — that we have no influence on our existence, no control over the circumstances we find ourselves in and that life merely happens to us. Not for us, and certainly not by us.

We expect that one day, when all the circumstances of our existence fall into place, and when we've worked hard enough, we will receive our rewards. And these rewards will bring with them the happiness that we've heard so much about. And so we toil in this endeavour, working harder, grinding away, awaiting everything that we are due. And when the rewards don't come, we find ourselves confused, bemused, bitter and angry. We find our circumstances growing darker and harder, work becomes drudgery, becomes back-breaking. We are dutifully following the path as it has been laid out for us, but it doesn't lead to the pot of gold we have been expecting.

If we are lucky, we will come to the realisation that we've have hung our hats on a misconception. We were told that if worked hard enough we would be rewarded with a good life of riches and happiness, but the truth is that we have it backwards. It is only once we are happy that we will find the good life and all its riches. Until then, until we are ready to receive our rewards, they will always remain out of reach and working harder and harder won't bring them any closer, despite what we've been led to believe.

We have been programmed with the wrong outlook, and our entire experience of life and the world we live in – our world – is a reflection of this outlook. It is a reflection of our beliefs and our attitudes. Indeed, almost everything we experience is, in one way or another, a reflection of us. If we are angry the world becomes hostile. If we feel constantly defeated the world surrounds us with impassable obstacles. If we are closed minded our world seems small.

But the world can be infinite if we dare to open our minds to new ways of seeing.

If we have a victim mentality, every way we turn we will find defeat, failure, enemies and traps to ensnare us. If we are blessed with confidence, we find ourselves relishing the challenges life offers us. If we lack self-esteem those challenges become insurmountable walls that seem impossible to overcome. If we look for beauty, we will find it. If we look for ugliness, we will find it.

Our world affirms our inner sense of self.

Our experience of the world is a reflection of our state of mind, and if we allow unfortunate instances, unkind people, or the hardships of our daily life grind us down, then they multiply. If we allow the traumas of our history to shape our present, then we will forever be trapped in the past where an ever-decreasing spiral will guide us down into the darkest recesses of our mind. Here our entire sense of identity – our entire self – becomes enmeshed with such a negative perspective that not even the brightest day can shine light on our mood. Not even the clearest skies can lift the fog of our perception.

But if we allow the beauty of the world, the joy of the potential it holds, and a love for all things good and wholesome to saturate our spirit, the world will smile back at us. Our world is a reflection of our state of being.

If we share love with the world, the world will love us back. If we embrace a joyful outlook our lives will fill with joy.

State of mind is fundamental to our experience of life, but it goes beyond simply adjusting our perspective so that we see things more positively. It is important to understand that when we adopt a positive energy within our psyche it has an influence in the real world. A good attitude leads to a good world around us – the things we can actually touch, observe and feel, become tangibly better. When we change internally, the world around us also changes – for real – in response to our new behaviours, attitudes and actions.

And the experience can be profound and addictive. The more change we see in response to our internal adjustments, the more we yearn to fine tune ourselves, and the more our world responds. We become the authors of our own lives and we discover intrinsic truths in the process. Truths such as this:

By letting go of what we desire, the things we desire find us.

It may seem like magic. In fact, when you transform your internal paradigms the world – and you – become magically alive. But it's quite a logical effect of a positive outlook. When your mind is closed and your perspective is focused on loss, lack and failure, that's all you will see. But when your perception is trained on beauty and abundance, when you are attuned to opportunities, and you live a life of intent, of mindful appreciation of the here and now, then you become aware of the smallest magic details that bring joy, ideas, and inspiration.

When you focus on everything that could and does go right, you become less dominated by the things that could and do go wrong. You take the hiccups, the misfortunes, the rainy days and the clouds that hang overhead in your stride, because you understand that they need not hold any power over you. And as a result, more things start to go your way than not. Life becomes filled with your successes, and even on the rainiest of days it feels as if the sun is shining. Because you are.

With every crunch of leaves underfoot, there is poetry. With every echoing footstep there is music. And with every eddy and flow of water and wind there is art. We find pleasure in the most unexpected places, find ourselves patient and calm in the most trying of circumstances, and find ourselves facing up to problems and challenges with zeal where previously we would have shied away or sought escape. We guide our awareness towards solutions instead of obstacles, to the good in every situation instead of the bad, to love instead of fear.

When we being to understand that it is our awareness that guides how we interact with and respond to the world around us, and that our awareness is almost entirely a tool for our own use, we can free ourselves from the manipulating forces that wish to control us – both externally and internally.

We learn to be guided by our own intentions, and that the actions of others – which so often lead to a reaction within us – need not have any control over us. Our responses come from within, our emotions come from within. We can feel how we choose to feel, respond how we wish to respond, no longer triggered, no longer reacting, no longer relinquishing responsibility for our state of mind and heart.

When something external makes us angry, we see that our anger comes from within. All along we have believed that external influences are responsible for the way we feel, but our feelings are just our own response to the stimulus of the outside world, or our own negative thoughts. Learning that our thoughts are not facts and that nobody can literally reach inside us and manipulate us, we can step aside from our usual reactions and choose responses that serve us better. We can choose dignity, magnanimity, mercy or kindness. We can choose not to waste our energy on emotions that cause us pain, but channel our focus somewhere else, onto something more positive that will have beneficial results in our life, and the lives of others.

By choosing not to waste our energy on these negative traits, which simply serve only to amplify the thing we believe caused them, we find ourselves in a better position to deal with situations, rather than being influenced and controlled by unnecessary emotional reactions and thoughts. Problems that previously seemed overwhelming can be tackled, previously daunting decisions are can be made effortlessly, and actions to craft life for the better can be undertaken.

Dramas become trifles. Crises become challenges. Everything gains a new perspective.

When we understand that we are not our thoughts, and that we are not their subject, we can free ourselves from their control, and regain the joy in life that negative thinking would otherwise deny us. We can choice our inputs, choose to pay attention to the things that trigger the kinds of feelings we wish to feel, and craft an existence of bliss, of confidence, of being someone that is empowered, content, and fully relishing everything that life has to offer.

We don't have to be angry. We don't have to be hurt. We don't have to be offended. We don't have to save face. We don't need to be afraid. We don't have to be proud. We can choose to use that energy for far more beneficial and interesting things instead.

All around us are experiences waiting to be seen, felt, enjoyed, relished, and endured. We can challenge ourselves to grow stronger through adversity, reward ourselves with vistas of beauty, and find magic in the smallest dew drops, the most mundane everyday things, and the tiniest of wonders that we would otherwise think insignificant or not even consider at all.

Our relationship with life is the relationship of the artist with their painting. And whether we realise it or not, our brush strokes have created the experience that we find ourselves having today. We are at the centre of a universe that extends outwards from us in every direction, and we are at the centre of every sorrow and every joy that we experience. We are the ones reading the poetry, singing those songs, or slogging through mud. We are the ones unable to accept our friends' successes, and we are the ones carrying the weight of the world on our shoulders. And we are the ones standing on the edge unsure whether we should fly or fall.

Our wanting deprives us of what we want. When we 'want' we are focused on what we are lacking, and this dissatisfaction keeps us trapped, unable to ever reach the thing we desire. Only by letting go of this desire, only by stopping wanting, can we truly reach the thing we seek the most. And we achieve this paradoxical goal by appreciating everything we have. Right here. Right now.

There is a life out there that is ours, that is different to the one we have now, but exists in parallel to it. And we can only find it when we stop hunting for it, and absorb ourselves into the blessings we already have. When we let go for a moment to look at our riches, we will find more riches drawn to us. We will find that we want for nothing, and that we are already wealthy beyond our dreams.

When we let go of that which is missing from our lives, we will find that nothing is missing. When we take time to focus on where we are, and what we've got, we will find ourselves right where we need to be, with nothing lacking. And the more we do this, the more we will find our dreams coming true. The more we focus on the joy we already have, the more joy will find us. The more we focus on the riches we are already blessed with, the more riches will find us. By letting go of wanting we get more of what we want.

When we become joyful, we find more joy. When we become loving, we find more love. When we embrace happiness, it embraces us back. And when we revel in our riches, our coffers overflow.

And what's more, none of this is metaphorical. The things we seek are seeking us, but they will only find us when the conditions are right. We can only find success when we celebrate the success we have already experienced, and applaud the success of others without any further agenda than love and support. The more we recognise the beauty in the world, the more beauty will find us until it surrounds us like a meadow of overgrown wildflowers. The more we adopt an attitude of kindness and generosity, the more the universe will reflect it back to us. The more we support others, the more we will find ourselves supported. The more we are interested in others the more interesting we become.

The more we reach out to greet people and pull them up, the more we will find hands to shake and pull us up too.

When our eyes and minds are opened to the magic of the world, we see that it has been here all along, just waiting for us to recognise it. And we will find our worlds become abundant and filled with meaning. Just as we have become abundant and filled with meaning.

By choosing gratitude over resentment and finding victories in even the smallest things on the darkest of days, we are able to weather the most tumultuous of storms, and come out the other side stronger, and more prepared for what fate will throw in our direction. And we will find that fate's slings and arrows seem more like mere trifles, and hidden among them are diamonds of opportunities, waiting for us to collect them as long as we are brave enough to push past the outrageous fortune.

Once past, on looking over our shoulder we might just glimpse our obstacles turning to dust, like Eurydice being snatched to the underworld, and we will wonder what stopped us in the first place.

When we open our arms, hearts and minds to embrace what life has to offer, we will find that we are embracing a better version of ourselves. And through our new intent, through our new intention to relish the joys that have already befallen us, we will find we have the power to choose a life that's more vivid, more real, and more authentic than anything we've ever experienced. Colours become sharper; textures become more defined. Life becomes infinitely more glorious.

We can choose to celebrate the victories of those around us as if they were our own. We can choose to face our own challenges with relish and zeal. We can choose to focus on the beauty of each drop of rain, each gust of wind, each falling leaf, and each hard-earned step through the uncharted adventure of our own, unique life. We can choose to celebrate love.

There are no maps here. There is no blueprint for a life well lived. So, we have to choose our own path. We can choose the rocky ground, or we can choose a route that will bring us beauty, opportunities, experiences, and a fulfilled potential. We can choose the path of fear or the path of love.

On the surface where we find ourselves from day to day, our confidence is dwarfed by our potential, and it is precisely this that leaves us cowering in the face of immense opportunity. But when our confidence rises up like a young sequoia to meet our capabilities for growth and achievement, we can soar like eagles, and become the brightest versions of ourselves possible.

It is up to us how brightly we wish to shine. But the brighter our light, the more we illuminate a world of possibilities for others. Isn't it time we realised what we are capable of, and created a world and a life that reflects everything we dream about?

If you shine brightly, the world will shine brightly back at you. So, shine.

Although I say
"Come here! Come here!" the fireflies
Keep flying away.

-     Uejima Onitsura

Chapter 4
The Reality of Other Worlds

"Below the threshold of consciousness everything was seething with life." – Karl Jung

We are pebbles, spinning, skipping, dancing along the water.

When we wake up in the morning, we wake into the surface world. This is the shallow land where we spend most of our time, and most of our effort. This is where the system of mankind exists, in which we are processed by the mechanisms of education, industrialism, capitalism and materialism.

This is the world of the tangible, the quantifiable, the political and the measurable.

This is where our jobs live, this is where bills must be paid, where the latest fashions exist to make us regard our wardrobes with dismay, and where our dissatisfaction is used as a tool to make us buy stuff, vote for stuff, and do stuff that is in the interests of others. This is the system that feeds off us, and it requires us to remain here, focused at all times on the things it wishes us to focus on, lest we awaken to the fact that there is something else, beyond this surface world, that is more powerful, more rewarding, and more fulfilling.

Advertising billboards say look here, look at this, don't look over there. Politicians and newspapers say, think this, be outraged by that, don't think for yourself. The industrialists say you will never be fulfilled, you will always be inadequate unless you buy our goods, wear our clothes, value 'things' above all else.

Keep your attention focused where the system of the shallow surface world needs you to look, and whatever you do don't look anywhere else but here. Don't dare to entertain notions of other worlds. All that is real and of any importance is here. All that exists is that which you can see with your own eyes and touch with your own hands and buy with your own money.

But we know better.

We are pebbles and we are spinning, skimming the surface, and whenever we touch the threshold and splash through – even if it's just for a moment – we get a glimpse of what lies beneath. If we are brave enough to open our eyes and look, we get hints of something else, other ways of seeing and other ways of being that exist in parallel to this surface world. These other places and other ideas can set us free from the shallow trappings of the surface world, offering us a level of perspective that diminishes its importance and its grasp on us, showing us ways to transcend it, master it, bend it to our will.

Some people never get this insight. These people never see below the surface, their pebbles flying in an arc clear of the water, and even if they do break through from time to time, they are so blind to what is in front of them – so unwilling to look – that it's as if they their eyes are closed. Only when their time in the surface world is finally done do they ultimately splash through the threshold with their eyes open. Only then do they see what they've been missing all along. Only then will they wish they could go back and do things differently. And depending on which tradition you follow, they may just get that chance – but their memory is unlikely to follow.

Most of us, though, break through the surface almost daily. We get glimpses when we sleep at night and our minds stray into dreams. We break through when we pause to contemplate a beautiful sunset, or the hypnotic tune of the bumblebees busying themselves on the lavender bush, or when we experience the endorphin-driven flow states of rhythmical exercise, when we create art, when we are moved by music, when we dance, or when we love.

Poetry, the feeling of the sun on our face, the sound of an owl at night, the brush stroke or chisel mark of the artist, the chef's mastery of flavours and the sound of the waves against the shore. All these things give us a peak below the surface. But we must be prepared to look.

The world of materialism wants all our attention all the time, because when our head is turned by these other, more captivating worlds, its value to us is diminished and its control over us weakens. If we spend too long exploring these other dimensions of our reality there is every chance that it may lose its grip on us altogether, and so it uses ploys and trickery to stop us straying from the course it intends for us.

The course it needs us to follow for its own sake.

We are taught to toe the line. To not rock the boat. We are instilled with mental roadblocks that hold us back, that tell us not to dare, not to spread our wings to fly, not to explore our potential, but to keep quiet and be subservient subjects rather than unique souls. Just as red traffic lights exert an imaginary force on us that makes us stop, we are encouraged to dismiss as fancy any indulgence of imagination, of thought, or dreams of fantasy.

Carry through these qualities into adulthood and it becomes a mental health concern, or we are labelled as hippies, outsiders, weirdos or followers of 'alternative lifestyles'. And so we bounce along, following guidelines and fences that don't exist anywhere but in our minds and the minds of our fellow humans. Surface-world abstractions such as the seven-day week, the twelve-month year or the twenty-four-hour day are made real by shared hallucination. But recognise that you are a spark in the darkness and the system becomes threatened. Step out of the shared hallucination and the system begins to break down.

At what point did being a unique and wild product of nature give way to being a uniform member of society with a social security number and a credit rating? How far can we go to regain our wild, animal freedom before an intervention is arranged?

Do we allow our children to dance freely or do we medicate them for ADHD? How many Jackson Pollock's have been told to stop making a mess and put their paints away? Would we tell George Gershwin to keep the noise down? By whose rules must we exist, other than our own? Everything else, every notion of what is deemed acceptable, correct, proper that is not of our own making is, surely, just an illusion imposed on us by other.

Our own ability to decide what is right or wrong, what is correct and normal, has been stolen from us and replaced with guide books, legislation, and written rules and regulations. These are vital to enable to system of the surface world to function efficiently and to weed out trouble makers, but in the process it has stolen from us our sense of responsibility and ability to create our own morality.

Where natural notions of right and wrong don't fit the extended value structures of the powers that be, notions of 'sin' and 'the rule of law' are introduced. Love between two of the wrong type becomes taboo, doing the moral thing gets replaced with obeying the law of the land. People get locked away for standing up for what is right and wholesome and true.

The system of the surface world aims to dominate and suppress our wild nature. It wants us to forgo our innate senses of love and kindness and gives us law books and regulations instead. It wants to tell us what to think and how to act. Coming together to dance in a field becomes subversive. Art and poetry threaten the status quo. Stopping to close your eyes and breathe becomes unusual, abnormal, dangerous.

But we are pebbles skimming the surface of the water, and when we woke this morning, we were blessed with new way of seeing. In our dreams we glimpsed below the surface, and saw that it was seething with life. And we brought a bit of it back with us when we returned, changed, reborn, baptised into a brighter reality.

We now find beauty where before we only saw mundanity. Where once we were enthralled by the latest pair of shoes, we are now entranced by raindrops gliding down the window. Where previously we were afraid to have thoughts of our own that weren't fed to us by the mass media, we now entertain ideas of travelling on light beams to the other side of the galaxy. When we see our friends and colleagues, we see their hopes and fears, their ambitions and their potential shimmering as if they are beings of pure energy. Which they are.

Where previously we were no more than the number on our passport or driving license, a consumer with a credit score, we are now sentient, dreaming creatures with energy flowing through us, and the grip the system has on us is starting to weaken. If we choose to open our eyes and our hearts, we can keep our feet in this world and let our souls fly to the edge of the universe and beyond, into the farthest reaches of the unimaginable.

With each skip we make across the surface our eyes open more to what lies beneath and upon our return to the shallow surface world of mankind's system, we bring a little more of what we've seen in that other place into this one. These visions and dreams take on mass and energy, and are waiting to become real.

But it is up to us to make them real. We can instead choose to forget what we saw in our dream state and brush our teeth, drink our coffee and get ready for work. We can choose to brush past the dew-jewelled spider's web without a second glance as we bring our mind back to this morning's meeting. We can forget where we've been, what we glimpsed and bring our entire being into the chores of the shallow surface world, sending our arc soaring high over the threshold, dismissing as nonsense or meaningless or unimportant anything that might hint at something deeper lying beneath.

Or we let it change us. We can pause before entering shops to buy more stuff, and give our attention just for a moment to the swaying of the blossom in the afternoon breeze, and decide that we don't need retail therapy after all. We can become fascinated by the bird in the tree as it preens itself, instead of losing ourselves in the infinite scroll of our handheld device. We can choose to shun the modern convenience of processed ready meals and explore instead the idea of growing and cooking our own food, and in doing so find a world of flavour opening up before us. We can leave the television switched off for an evening to talk, or read, or make art, and the advertisers yearn for our attention, which they no longer hold.

We can choose to engage with the life that surround us. The life we are a part of.

If we simply stop to look around us, our world grows before our very eyes. Colours become richer, textures more visceral and everything becomes an adventure of sensation and indulgence. Art becomes a portal to another world, colour becomes luxurious and the world that was once familiar is now strange, enthralling and pulsating with energy.

We all want this. A part of us aches for it. Crowds flock to see the cherry blossom in Japan, to swim with dolphins in azure seas, to lose themselves in ballet, to find escape in country walks or to gaze up in silence at star-filled skies.

If we are brave enough to look, we can find this escape wherever we go, and dip below the surface at will. We can remove ourselves from the insignificant mediocrity of the material world by noticing shadows, appreciating contours, or simply pausing to breathe with intent. We are engaged with our senses and our world is richer, more colourful, more rewarding than it was before. We find ourselves wealthy, wanting for less — if anything — because we recognise the abundance that surrounds us.

The urge to buy more lessens. Our money stays in our pockets. And we are richer in every way.

Our senses are never switched off. Even when we sleep, we are listening for the dangers of the jungle, the approaching tiger, or the creeping lion. Our brain decides what to make us aware of and wake us, or what it can let pass and allow us to rest. Indeed, we are conscious of just a small amount of the information we receive. Our skin detects minute fluctuations in temperature and air pressure, we hear things we don't consciously register, and we see things in our peripheral vision that we pay no notice to.

But while we choose not to be aware of these things, our subconscious processes it all and feeds this information to our intuition. Like a guiding voice it whispers and hints to us, yet in the past these words went unnoticed. But now that we have become tuned in to other ways of seeing, other worlds, the vibrant textures of thought and the experiences that the universes without and within have to offer, we find ourselves more aligned to our intuitive capabilities.

We are attuned to the emotions of others, to our ability to read situations, to our ability to feel. We become awed by the smallest of things, the sound of a baby breathing, the sensation of movement, and even the passing of time from moment to moment. Our very sense of the here and now is alive and bursting with energy. And we are the centre of it all.

And we know that this is nothing new, but something that's been with us since we were in the womb. But in the days and years that have passed, this innate ability to explore these worlds, to traverse time and space, to converse with the spirits of those long past, of those not yet born, and those who won't ever exist, has become calcified by the guidelines and rules of the shallow surface world.

Where once we dreamed of touching the heavens, we now figure out payment plans to clear our overdrafts. Where once we splashed and danced in muddy puddles, we now take care not to get our suits wet. Where once we made up songs about flying, we now keep quiet in case anybody notices us.

But as we start to engage with our awareness, we begin to rediscover the gifts that we were born with. The magic of sight that relies not on eyes, but on freedom from rules. Nothing is impossible unless we believe it to be, and now we can see again anything and everything becomes possible. The withered belief structures imposed on us by convention, tradition and culture are turning to dust, and in their place we stand, at the centre of an infinite universe that is ours. And from here the shallow surface world is humbled, and bends to our will.

We are no longer its servants, but it is ours. All we need is faith in our new-found freedom, and the resolve to never let our vision be distorted again. Life happens for us, not to us. We don't work for the system; it works for us. But only if we are willing to make it so.

A world of dew,
Is a world of dew, and yet
And yet...

—   Kobayashi Issa

Chapter 5
A Continuum of Being

"The moment you doubt whether you can fly, you cease forever to be able to do it." – **J.M. Barrie**

From where we are now, at this precise moment, the infinite universe stretches out in every direction. And we – each of us, individually – are at the very centre of it. It is impossible for anyone else to be at the centre of the universe because we can only ever experience it for ourselves, from this time and place. We are, therefore, not only at the centre of the universe, but the universe is ours and ours alone. And it not only exists, but it exists for us, and us alone.

The universe is infinite and we, as part of it, are infinite too.

Other people inhabit our infinite universe, just as we inhabit theirs. From where they are, at this very moment, they are at the centre of their infinite universe, and it spreads out from them in all directions. And you are a guest in it, just as they are a guest in yours.

From each of us, an infinite number of ethereal threads connect us to everyone and everything. Through our experiences, the experiences of others, the paths we cross and the ideas and dreams that we imagine, everything that has happened, could happen, is happening – or could never possibly happen – *is* happening, and we are connected to it in this instant.

When we pick up a book, we are connected to the tree whose wood was used to make the paper, the soil from which it grew from seed to sapling to towering birch, and all the animals and people that took shelter in the shade of its branches. We are connected to the papermakers, the book binders and the printers who used their skills to turn that tree into the book that you hold in your hands. We are connected to the floor they stood on, the breakfast they ate, the calluses on their skilled hands, and the years of training, of life, of love, of hurt and of joy, that they have experienced.

Ethereal threads reach through the book and its pages, as if it were a portal that connects us to everyone involved in its making, everyone who has ever touched it, distributed it, leafed through its pages. The ethereal threads connect us to their lives, their dreams, all the things that made them real, and all the things that they imagined. And in doing so they are real now, today, right here, even if their time was two hundred years ago.

When we start to read the words printed on the pages, we are connected to the writer as they sat at their desk. We are joined with their thought processes, everything they went through when imagining the words that would become the sentences in their books. We are there, sat beside them as they struggle with writers' block, as they tap their pencil on the desk, gazing out of the window, hoping that inspiration will strike them, and that final chapter will take form.

We are connected to the characters in their book as if they were real people. Their dreams, their motivations, the reality of their imagined existence. Their loves, their sorrows, and how their lives take form in our imaginations after we put the book down, but their story lingers in our mind for time to come.

These ethereal threads connect us to the writer through space, through time, and through imagination and ideas, and they connect the writer to us. As you read this you, we – you and I – are connected through time and space. You are here with me now as I sit at my desk typing out this chapter, you are with me as I wonder where it will fit with the other chapters of the book, as I consider what time I'll get to sleep tonight, if I'll make it to the train station on time, if anyone will ever read this and it if it makes any sense at all. Our ethereal threads are entangled, invisible, but as real as we decide to make them.

When we put our books down and step out into the sunshine to walk on the earth we are connected to the planet, it's place in the cosmos, and everyone who has ever walked under the same sky, looked up at the same moon, and dug for riches beneath its surface. We are at the centre of our universe, and it stretches out in every direction from us, backwards and forwards through time. And we are part of this continuum of being, connected to everything by our ethereal threads.

These threads enable us to travel to the far reaches of the universe. They enable us to experience the impossible. We can be anyone or anything and anywhere we wish to be, by following the correct thread and seeing where it will take us. Our threads can show us what the Sultan of Brunei is thinking, they can show us the emotions our cat would feel if it was to float away in a bubble, or what the food tasted like in the dining room of King Henry VIII.

These ideas, daydreams and explorations are the result of electrochemical pulses that travel along our neurones. These are the same pulses that allow us to move our legs and chew our food, but when they fire at a different frequency along a different pathway they become signals that allow us to use our voices to communicate, to nod our heads and to smile in agreement. At yet another frequency the pulses become dreams while we sleep, ideas for the future, inspiration, ideas, roadmaps to something better, or to self-destruction.

And just as our thoughts have a frequency, so does everything else in the universe. From the rotation of the planets around the sun, to the strings of a violin, to the atoms in a glass of water. If you look closely enough you can observe the electrons, the protons and neutrons vibrating furiously, and the more energy they become charged with the more furious their vibrations become. When you look closely enough boundaries breakdown, and at the sub-atomic level it's impossible to see where your atoms end and the atoms in the chair you're sitting on begin. Where the atoms of your feet end and the atoms of the earth begin. All we see are vibrations, energy made manifest. When broken down into its smallest parts energy is all that remains, and that is all we are. We are vibrating energy, in an infinite sea of vibrating energy. We are, therefore, as infinite as the ocean to which we belong, part of a continuum of being. As a wave is to the sea.

Bring together two objects that are vibrating at similar frequencies, and the weaker vibration will adjust itself and harmonise with the stronger. When tuning forks are brought together their frequencies align. When the frequency of an opera singer's voice matches the natural frequency of a wine glass the glass can begin to vibrate and sing too. If the singer's voice becomes too powerful the glass can break, a phenomenon that has also been seen when earthquakes topple some buildings but not others, or when, in 1940, a fierce wind matched the natural frequency of the Tacoma Narrows Bridge. As the wind blew through the structure of the giant suspension bridge it began to swing, gaining momentum until finally it the frequency became too strong and the bridge broke apart and collapsed.

Strong frequencies can have powerful effects. Microwave radiation agitates water molecules, causing them to heat up, and can be used to cook food. Other types of radiation have frequencies that can be damaging to human cells, or can transmit signals through the air to our televisions, or to satellites far out in space.

Strong ideas can also harmonise in the minds of others. Pictures and stories created in the minds of artists, authors and musicians, can resonate in the minds of those who are willing to listen. But just like the wine glass that shatters, or the bridge that collapses, the resonance of ideas can also be damaging. When people who are lost are given an enemy to blame for their own unfortunate circumstances, the boundaries between good and evil can break down as the stronger frequencies force the weaker to harmonise with them and people forget which thoughts are their own and which have been placed there by others.

Ideas of hate resonate strongly, and when people's own vibrations are low — when they are tired, lost, desperate or confused — it is easy for these ideas to harmonise in the minds of those who yearn for clarity, relief and a focus for their negativity. From here anger and bitterness and resentment become racism, misogyny, bigotry and other manifestations of fear. Hate is the junk food of the soul. It provides a tasty treat right now, but it is lacking in nourishment and will ultimately starve our souls.

We are all transmitting at a frequency of a certain energy. And there is always a chance that our frequency will harmonise with others, or theirs will harmonise with ours. Much better that we choose good energy to harmonise with. Frequencies of hope, of kindness, of opportunity and beauty. Frequencies of togetherness and betterment.

Our vibrations radiate outwards, and together with the vibrations of every person on the planet, every object and atom in the universe, they combine to form the resonance of this infinite continuum of being that permeates every inch of this plain of existence. We all have the opportunity to raise this universal frequency by raising our own. What you think today, what you do tomorrow, how gently and kindly you live, these actions have a frequency that influences the universe that stretches out in every direction from you, that influences all the ethereal threads that connect you to everyone and everything, that influences what your universe will look like tomorrow. And it influences everyone else's universes too.

Appreciate beauty and it thrives. Engage in hate and that flourishes too. One builds, and the other destroys.

It's important that you vibrate at a high frequency, so that others might harmonise with you, to raise the frequency of our continuum of being. Be the change that you want to see in the world, and the world will come to meet you.

This mallet –
Long ago was it a camellia?
A plum tree?

— Matsuo Bashō

Chapter 6
Our Capacity

"The narcissism of small differences is a seduction that keeps us from focusing on real value by doing important work." – **Seth Godin**

Our potential is limitless. There is nothing we can't achieve, in either our consideration of ideas and our understanding of the infinite universe that surrounds us, or in our ability to do great things and change the course of human history. We can set foot on the moon, send machines to the far reaches of the solar system, learn the languages of cultures on the other side of the planet, and create amazing, wonderful things – works of art, accomplishments of science and engineering, revolutions and step changes in human understanding and knowledge. We can communicate, elucidate, and educate.

We have the capacity to find god in the first of the season's apple blossom, and music in the babble of a fast-flowing stream. We can feel moved by the lowing of cattle, and find ourselves touched deeply by a sunset, by the sound of rain against the window, a train in the distance, or the wind as it blows the autumn leaves around the garden.

We have a vast capacity for imagination that can guide our actions to achieve great things in this world, or lead us to great visions in the other worlds of dreams and thought. We imagine the lives of strangers as we people-watch from the café in the square, and when we let our imagination flow as we sleep or daydream, we can transport ourselves to other worlds. Worlds where we converse with the great poets, or fly uninhibited by the laws of physics, the rules of man, or the influence of others, or where we touch down on far-off planets that exist only in our mind's eye.

When we set ourselves free like this we can go anywhere, be anyone and do anything. We can live lives that we never thought someone 'like us' could achieve, because we have shed the shackles of doubt and given ourselves permission to dare. We can touch the lives of others, share our fire so that their own paths may be illuminated and make the world a brighter place.

But more than this, if we can suspend our disbelief long enough, we can drag our dreams back into this shallow, surface world. All of this is possible, if we allow it to happen. All of this can be real, if we use our capacity wisely, for greatness, for free thinking, and for empowerment.

But dreaming doesn't serve the system of the shallow surface world, and all too often we find ourselves using up our capacity with other things – distractions that keep us from living. Things of the surface world, shallow and unbecoming, ugly and all-consuming. Things that serve to tie us down, keep us trapped, our wings clipped to prevent us from flying.

In the surface world of shallow things, we are lured into using our capacity for hatred instead of love, insecurity instead of confidence, for small matters instead of infinite, and to be trapped by the illusions of fear instilled within us by people who gain when we don't spread our wings. We are told we will never be enough unless we buy this thing or that, and we are told it over and over, until our sense of identity is so attached to the thing that we must have – as well as the sense of emptiness born of not having it – that we surrender our capacity to the notion of material desires.

Similarly, we are told to be afraid, that we are experiencing this state of lack – of inadequacy – because it is being kept from us by others. These others will do us harm, and they will take more and more until we have nothing left, until we are nobody. We are told to be afraid of these others, some of whom live among us, some of whom live outside the city walls, and we must defend ourselves at all costs.

We are told to fear anyone who doesn't conform to the tick-boxes of the system. Anyone who doesn't fit in. Anyone who is different. Foreign. Alien. Strange or unusual.

And we either find ourselves overtaken by the fear that they wish us to feel and, brainwashed, that we vote for their divisive, inhuman, hate-fuelled politics, or we find ourselves offended by them, outraged, defensive, and we reflect their hatred right back at them with added gusto and vitriol. Disgusted, and shocked, and in utter contempt, our capacity filled up with anger and rage and hatred whichever side of this dirty no-man's land we find ourselves on.

And our capacity? Full. Full of prejudice, full of anger, full of hate and poison and distraction. Unable to fly we find ourselves trapped by notions of national borders, terrified that everything we believe in is under threat from one enemy or another, determined to use what energy we have to fight this dark force that threatens our beautiful land.

The system requires us to be afraid and in a state of lack, so it finds us things to fear. Because when we're frightened, we don't think for ourselves. We are distracted, preoccupied, and we don't challenge the way things are, simply because that's how they have always been. It's our bedrock.

Even our everyday life is – they would have us believe – the enemy. We should be afraid of the earth we walk on and the bacteria that live in it, afraid of the air we breathe, afraid of the food we eat, afraid of anything that isn't processed, packaged, capitalised upon. Our streets are awash with the blood of crime victims, so we'd better stay indoors and watch the television news and the soap operas. Our food is poisoned, the carrots we try to grow ourselves are the wrong shape, the soil is toxic, so it's best that we buy their pre-prepared, sterilised, pasteurised, homogenised, standardised fare. Line their pockets and they will keep us safe, docile, protected from the foreigners, from the other, from the outdoors, and they will pump our minds and our bodies full of their preservatives, their propaganda and their own intentions.

We are no longer humans but consumers, to be managed, milked for our cash like dairy cows, kept in a state of constant lack, of fear, of want, of disgust, of conflict and adversity. Orwell's two-minute hate is the new national anthem and our screams of fear and aggression sound like cash registers to those who look on, counting their money with dirty fingers.

And all along we're being hoodwinked. While we stand on one side of the battlefield or the other, afraid and disgusted that what we eat might kills us, that who we meet might kill us, that crossing the street might kill us, we miss another way of being. This other way doesn't serve the system or those who profit from it — it serves us — so they try to lure us away from it, tell us not to look at it, and draw the curtains, hiding it from sight.

But this other way offers us an alternative to this shallow surface world of consumerism and pre-digested newsbites, to anger, conflict and tribalism. This other way asks us to pause for a moment and listen, because life itself is calling us, and all we need to do is turn our attention towards it, release our grasp on superficial distractions, and the doors to new worlds will open before us.

Because if you step away from the heaving, screaming masses for a moment, back away from the clawing hands grabbing at Black Friday bargains, turn away from the flying fists of tribalism and prejudice, and look down, you might just notice a blade of grass forcing its way through a crack in the pavement. Above it a thousand angels are beckoning it, urging it to fulfil its potential and "grow, grow." Listen carefully and you might just hear it straining as it pushes to be all it can be, and reaches towards the sky.

If you look up, you might notice the shooting stars animating the immaculate heavens. Their fiery tails becoming paths through the cosmos, showing dreamers the way forward, and carrying wishes into the ether as the moon looks on.

If you look to your side you might see the outstretched hands of those fleeing conflict and torment, poverty and famine, anxiety, insecurity and struggles, those seeking your help if you could only reach out and pull them up. Those who, despite the different colour of their skin, the different languages they speak, the looks of desperation in their eyes and the dirt under their fingernails, are just like you.

And if you look to your other side, you might see the outstretched hands of those who want to help you, who would share opportunities if you would just let them pull you up. Those who offer the chance of a better life, of release from dissatisfaction, of a life of not wanting for anything, of joy, bliss, peace, collaboration and contentment.

We are distracted by ideas that aren't our own, which are easy to hold on to because they spare us the hard work of thinking for ourselves. If we were to choose our own thoughts, we could see that national borders are just cages to keep the narrow-minded enslaved, trapped with their own fear. Alone, petrified in the dark.

If we were to think for ourselves, we would see that we don't need to pay the system with our self-esteem in order to get a sense of our own identity and worth, and

we would realise that feeling good about ourselves —
about who we are — is in itself a rebellious act of
emancipation.

And if we were to think for ourselves, we would find
that we have an untapped capacity for dreaming, for
doing, for creating, and for achieving anything we want.
Nobody can convince us not to, because they no longer
control our thinking. We don't need permission,
validation, or the approval of others. We need
empowerment, and that comes from within.

When we understand that we no longer need to be told
what to think, but we must learn to think for ourselves,
we begin to discover who we are. We begin to realise
that it's not somebody else's life that we need, but we
need to create a life of our own. We can feed ourselves.
We can stop yearning for the clothes, the cars, the
material frivolities of others to validate our sense of
worth because that validation comes from inside us.
When somebody else achieves a level of success, we
don't take it personally as a reflection of our own
failure, we don't feel bitter, we don't think that we are
in any way lessened by what they have done, because
we no longer need to compare ourselves with the
benchmarks of the outside world.

And when we are no longer being told what to think, we
find that we are no longer captivated by fear, and
instead discover a capacity to love. We can start to
celebrate the successes of others as if they were our
own, we can start to encourage others to realise their
dreams, and we can start to feel good about ourselves,
despite what is happening to other people.

The world becomes our playground.

The more we explore, the more we play, the more we see just how far we can push and stretch and twist this thing, the more we free our capacity to do great things. We begin to skip from one fantasy to the next, as we meander gleefully around the vast landscape of our potential, finding things to see, things to do, experiences to have, and ultimately discovering our calling.

New worlds offer themselves to us through art and literature and play. And underlying it all is a sense of joyfulness, of love and compassion, of a snowballing positive energy that grows stronger the more we recognise just how wonderful even the most minute details of this life are. Pebbles become diamonds, planes flying overhead become circling dragons, and the gentle sound of the shishi-odoshi reminds us of the passing of time, bringing us back to the present moment with its dull thud and splashing percussion.

Freed from the ideas that others wish us to think, freed from the expectations that we place upon ourselves, and freed from the boundaries of convention and tradition, we find ourselves confronting a blank page. Like artists we are faced with an opportunity to create something new, we find ourselves on the cusp of being reborn, and our world – our reality – along with us.

This is our time, and it's passing second by second. Empowered to think for ourselves, free to be who we want to be rather than who we think we're supposed to be, we find ourselves faced with an opportunity and a huge responsibility. Will we revert to our old ways and seek masks to hide behind, excuses to protect us from engaging with everything the universe has to offer, and the responsibility and risk that comes from being our ultimate selves, or will we launch ourselves into the unknown?

Will we fill these pristine blank pages with a new story that has, until now, remained unwritten? Will we see where this adventure will take us? Or will we keep telling ourselves the old familiar tale that has brought us this far, but will keep us here if we let it? Will we be brave enough to become the heroes of our story, or will we hide behind clichés and tales of woe to prevent so that we don't have to realise our true worth.

Now is our time. It has always been our time. And unless we step up and embrace the beauty and the opportunity, it will pass us by. How long will we allow it to slip through our fingers like the grains of sand in an hourglass? How many more glorious sunrises will we sleep through? What do we expect of the next life, that this life is so unimportant for us to engage with an make the most of? When will we start dancing to the music that's been playing all along?

Everything we've been given is for us, yet we give it away to others as if it were a red-hot coal. We live for the expectations of others, we give our thinking over to others, we give our values over to others, and we live the lives we think other people want us to live. We give away our lives so readily that anyone would think we're afraid of living, yet this life that we've been blessed with is the greatest gift of all.

We are artists, and we have the choice of making life our masterpiece, or passing the brush to someone else and allowing them to spoil our canvas. We can choose to paint freely and joyously with all the colours of the rainbow, or we can paint inside the lines drawn out by others. We can make this life our own, or we can be extras in someone else's story.

We all have the capacity to do great things. Why don't we?

The wonder of flowers
opening
and birds singing:
prayers!

— Gozan

Chapter 7
The Boy and the Forest

"The Universe is full of magical things, patiently waiting for our wits to grow sharper." – **Eden Phillpotts**

Turning it over in the palm of his hand the boy studied the tiny seed. Shaped like a teardrop, but bone dry in his palm, he couldn't fathom how something a small as this could become a giant sequoia. Yet that's what his grandad had told him when he had pressed it into his hand a week ago, making him promise to plant it as soon as he got a chance.

Now with grandad gone and no reason to remain, he knew it was the time to cross the desert and become the grown man that his destiny demanded. The next chapter of his life awaited, and he couldn't wait to begin, but not before he had fulfilled his grandfather's wishes.

He looked out across the arid desert, shielding his eyes against the unforgiving sun and the sand that blew sharply in the wind. The heat could play tricks on you out here, its shimmer creating spectres and illusions in the light. For a moment he thought he saw the figure of a person on the horizon. But he had grown up around these treacherous sands and was familiar with the tricks of the dunes. He knew how they could lure you to your death if you weren't familiar with their ways, and how they could send you mad if you didn't die of thirst first.

But these sands had been his playground, and his grandad had shown him their ways. He knew how to find water and make shelter should he ever become lost. He knew how to navigate their shifting topography. He knew how to traverse them safely without a second thought, while others would perish in a matter of hours.

Looking again into the distance, the figure reappeared, more visible now in the radiant heat, which danced and made shapes in the air. Clearly a fellow desert dweller, whoever this was seemed unperturbed by the heat and the flies and the sand.

Turning his attention back to the sequoia seed, the boy knelt down and started to dig a hole in the sand. Deeper through the sand he dug, until it became dry earth. Just a little deeper and the earth began to get a little moist. He'd chosen this spot well.

Dropping the seed into the hole he covered it over, piling on top of it earth and then sand until there was no sign of the seed's resting place. Reaching into his pack he pulled out a leather flask, untied its neck and took a sip, before emptying the rest onto the spot where he had buried the seed.

"A sip if you may," a voice from behind him called out. The boy turned and the figure who he had seen approaching through the shimmering heat was made manifest in front of him, and the old step closer, his hand outstretched. The boy handed him the flask and the man raised it to his lips to catch the last drops before handing it back.

"Just enough to wet the whistle," said the man, observing the boy. "What are you up to here?"

The boy looked up at the man, who was buried underneath layers of shawls and robes. He had clearly been travelling for a long time, and the lines on his face suggested a lifetime of adventures and stories and things that the boy was eager to see for himself.

"I'm planting a forest," replied the boy. "And then I'm crossing the desert to make a life for myself."

The old man smiled and turned to look in the direction he had just come from. He thought for a moment of the things he'd seen, the encounters and the stories, the experiences and the poetry, the excitement, the love and the laughter. He savoured the memories for a moment before turning back to the boy.

"And what a life you will have. But make sure you hold on to as much of it as you can, so that when you return to your forest, you'll be able to reflect on what a wonderful life it has been," and the old man leaned towards the boy. He recognised something in his eyes, in the unwrinkled skin and the twinkle of yearning for adventure. "I've come a long, long way. My bones ache, and my feet are sore. I've been walking my whole life. Do you mind, young man, if I pause for a moment in the shade of your forest?"

Clearly the heat of the desert had affected this strange old man, thought the boy. But who was he to deprive a tired, deluded old man the comfort of his delusion?

"Of course," he said, and picking up his bag he bade the man farewell and set off on his journey. After ten minutes and few hundred meters he turned and saw the old man sitting in the sand with his eyes closed, barely visible in the haze. He couldn't tell if he was dead or just sleeping, and for a moment the shimmering heat that rose above him conjured an illusion of the tallest of trees reaching into the sky.

The boy observed the mirage, and then turned to continue his journey. He walked and he walked, until the desert turned to grassland. For some months he fended for himself, feeding off the land and living in nature's lap. Everything he ever wanted was provided for him, and all he needed was to reach out and get it.

Eventually he came to a village where he became the apprentice of the local blacksmith and learned the ways of metal. He became skilled at shoeing horses, at making swords and armour. And one day, after several years and when he was no longer a boy or an apprentice, the young man packed up a suit of armour and a sword that he had made for himself, said goodbye to his mentor and set off to find his fortune.

After weeks of travelling he came upon the camp of a Ronin. The masterless samurai, himself seeking fortune on his travels observed the stranger's sword sticking out of his pack, and took it upon himself to pass on his skills to this interesting man, who soon became his friend and student. The man, eager to embrace everything that life could offer, travelled with the Ronin for several years, soaking up everything he could as the two of them became swords-for-hire, helping the helpless who needed their services – for the right price.

Eventually the old Ronin grew weary and chose to hang up his sword, and they parted ways, his student moving on to the next part of his adventure. The years went by and he was no longer a young man, but always remained a student, and everyone he met became his teacher. He fell in love and married, settled down and set up a business. Fortune soon followed, and followed by bust some years later, and fortune again.

As the decades passed and took their toll on both their bodies, eventually his wife succumbed to the passing of time and departed him. Broken hearted, he sobbed at her graveside, and as his tears fell onto the soil he was reminded of his last day of childhood and the sequoia seed his grandfather had given him. With no reason to remain, he sold all his possessions and packing up the essentials into a sack bag, he set off to return to the desert.

For more than a year he trekked back the way he had come. Through the plains he had traversed as a mercenary swordsman, through the wilds that had fed and watered him, and through the village where he had mastered metal. Until he arrived at the edge of the desert, and its baking heat.

As he walked through the sands and traversed the dunes, the skills he had grown up with, which had been taught to him by his grandfather came flooding back. For the untrained the heat and the shimmer of the desert could cause madness, but he knew not to be fooled by their ways.

But then he saw the shimmer stretching into the sky, and in the distance it appeared as a forest reaching into the heavens. He rubbed his eyes, and the longer he walked the more real the forest became, taller, more vivid, the illusion near perfect as it waved in front of him. Perhaps, he thought, he'd been away too long, and he swore he saw birds flying among the branches, squirrels climbing up their trunks, and the sound of woodpeckers and owls echoing out toward him across the sand.

Eventually the shimmering solidified, and the forest became real, reaching infinitely into the sky, and as far as the eye could see in all directions. And there in front of him stood a boy pouring water from a flask onto the soil.

"A sip if you may," he reached out, praying there was a little left in the leather flask to soothe his parched lips. The boy handed it to him, and he wet his mouth gratefully with the last few drops.

They observed each other cautiously, but in the boy he saw something familiar. There was something that reminded him of himself, something that had been a part of him a long time ago, which had never left, but which lay dormant like a seed in arid ground. He asked the boy what he was doing.

"I'm planting a forest," came the answer, and then the youngster told him he was off to find his fortune and live his life. The old man paused for a while, and looking up into the canopy of the giant sequoia the towered above him thought that this would be a good place to stop for a while. He leaned forwards.

"I've come a long, long way," he said to the boy. "My bones ache, and my feet are sore. I've been walking my whole life. Do you mind, young man, if I pause for a moment in the shade of your forest?"

The boy gave him a quizzical look before beckoning him to sit beneath the trees, and then he picked up his bag and set off across the sands. The old man sat down wearily at the base of a particularly huge tree and leant back against its trunk. Closing his eyes, he thought of the adventures he'd had. The things he'd seen, the people he'd met and the stories he could tell. Right now, though, he just wanted a little rest. Just a few minutes to snooze in the shade of this beautiful forest.

He closed his eyes. And just for a moment or two, allowed himself to drift off to the sound of birds singing above him in the leaves.

After a few hundred meters of walking the boy turned and saw the old man sitting in the sand with his eyes closed, barely visible in the haze. And for a moment the shimmering heat that stretched above him resembled the tallest of trees reaching into the sky.

First autumn morning:
The mirror I stare into
Shows my father's face.

-    Murakami Kijo

Chapter 8
The Way We See Things

"Reality is created by the mind. We can change our reality by changing our mind." – Plato

What you focus on expands, says the adage, and there it is — the truth about the world we inhabit. Different for all of us, distorted by our preoccupations and our preconceptions, we see only that which we are attuned to see, and it is this perspective that influences who we are, how we behave, and therefore the shape of the life we live.

A gardener exists in a world of flowers, whereas a builder exists in a world of bricks. It's the same world, under the same sky, yet their focus and their paradigms define how it appears to them – and therefore the way they behave. This in turn drives the spiral further and the self-fulfilling prophecy is set in motion.

When we look at our environment what we see are our biases and our internal stories — the things that we've been taught to believe about ourselves and the world around us. We see the broken relationships and abuse of our past, we see what we've been taught, through years of experience, to see. If we read the news, we see ourselves surrounded by danger. When we see successful people, we often believe that 'people like us don't have lives like that.'

If we have spent our lives being told that our opinion means nothing, we stop having an opinion, stop making decisions and find ourselves unable to participate in the life that is going on around us, in all its technicolour glory. If we been brought up to see the beauty of the world, then we revel in the joy of the warmest sunset and find ourselves surrounded by the most wonderful things this technicolour life has to offer.

If our experience of dogs is of being bitten, then we will be afraid of them. But if our experience of dogs is of cuddly puppies, we will see dogs in an entirely different way. Dogs are dogs, but our perspective has changed.

If we have been programmed or, worse, if we have programmed ourselves to see danger everywhere, the world will be frightening and overflowing with risk. If we've been programmed to recognise opportunities, we will see the world as a buffet of choice. Some may taste good and some may taste bad, but the choice is ours, if we're not too frightened to approach the table.

The same is true when we look in the mirror. Have we trained ourselves to focus in on our flaws and the things we like the least, or have we trained ourselves to see those good things? Instead of seeing the wrinkles around our eyes, do we choose to see how warm and friendly our gaze is? Instead of standing hunched and withered, do we choose to stand up straight and strong?

Anais Nin stated that "we don't see the world as it is, we see the world as we are", and within this statement lies a profound magic. If we can change our inner programming, we can change the world around us. A new state of mind can deliver a new perspective on life. If we were to start showing others the kind of respect we would wish to receive, would the world reflect it back to us? If we were to start loving ourselves, could we love the world more? When we step up to life, it steps up to meet us, and we can either grasp it with both hands, or we can let it slip away like grains of sand through our fingers.

Do we choose to dance, or do we sit on the sidelines convinced that we cannot? Do we dip our toe in the water, or do we walk away because we've convinced ourselves we can't swim? Do we step outside the front door and take a breath, or do we stay indoors because we believe it's much safer in here?

We live in a cage of our own making, and as the creators of this cage we can either choose to be its prisoners or its masters. We can choose to let the walls fall away and reveal the infinite plains of a life of opportunity, or we can stare at the bricks, convinced they're immovable, not daring to so much as sneeze lest they wobble.

By choosing to undo our programming and rewrite our stories, we can teach ourselves to see the world in a way that is much more favourable to us. By rewording the messages we tell ourselves, and by refusing to be held captive by our negative thinking, our negative past experiences, and the things that have so far failed to bring us the happiness and joy that we would like to see in our lives, we can bend reality to our will. We can choose to see obstacles as opportunities, sunshine on a cloudy day, and to tackle our fears head on until they crumble before us.

We can choose to focus on beauty, and as we do it will expand until it fills our vision. We can choose to focus on the characteristics within ourselves that we are proud of, rather than fixating on our flaws, and our confidence will grow. We can choose to focus on love and compassion, and in doing so it will expand until we find it impossible to think badly of others, impossible to judge and complain, and our world will become one of love, understanding and warm, welcoming friendliness.

We can steer our ship away from the darkest weather, but only if we choose to take the rudder. We can escape the swirling maelstrom that has kept us trapped within the storm, but only if we use intent to plot a course to fairer seas. The ocean that we float on can cradle us and rock us gently as it transports us to magical new worlds, but we must believe that it can, or we will never undertake the endeavour to escape the crashing waves that we have endured our entire lives.

Calm seas ne'er a good sailor make, they say, and we've had our fair share of turbulent tides, but now it's time to bring our ship home to happiness and contentment. It can be done, you can do it, but it requires commitment, an open mind, and the determination to taste the fruits of dry land.

Yes, we've had our difficulties, our upsets and our traumas. But we can either look at them as something that we drag behind us like a great weight, or we can use them as something that can make us stronger, better, more compassionate, and more confident. We can share the lessons that our hardships have taught us, and help others to find their strength too. We can choose who we want to be, by focusing on the behaviours and the mental characteristics that will make us better, and in turn our world will become better too.

Changing the way we look at the world, ourselves and our life doesn't simply affect our perspective, but it actually changes our world, ourselves and our life. If we focus on behaving with more confidence, we become more confident, and the results we experience will be those of someone with confidence. If we focus on becoming the kind of person who leans toward action rather than inaction – and in doing so, take action – then we will reap the rewards of those actions.

The way we perceive things, the stories we tell ourselves, and the refusal to simply sit back and let the world impose itself upon us are key to becoming who we want to be and living the lives we wish to live. If we want a better job, we need to change our perspective in order to make it realistic in our own belief system. Instead of telling ourselves "people like us don't have lives like that" we need to change the conversation.

People like us can have lives like that. People like us do have lives like that. People like us aren't afraid to take the steps necessary to make it happen. And sometimes those steps require critical reflections upon those personal traits of ours that we consider to be true, and even hold dear, but which may be holding us back.

If we can be brave enough to recognise our self-defeating self-talk, to understand that constantly sabotaging our own chances and virtues is skewing our perspective of ourselves and our environment, and also be brave enough to identify our shortcomings and work to overcome them, then people like us can have lives like that.

When we shed the self-defeating narrative of our lives, when we thank the events of our past – both good and bad – for the lessons they've taught us and the tools they've given us, and let them go, we can start to recreate our existence the way we would like it. We can start to take the action necessary to become the people we want to be, to do the things required to build the life we want to live.

When we decide to focus on all that's good, instead of all that's bad, we find ourselves surrounded by goodness. When we decide to stop listening to the undermining thoughts in our head, and instead use our mental capacity for more productive tasks, we can take ownership of our story. When we stop living in fear, we can do anything.

The lamp once out
Cool stars enter
The window frame.

— Natsume Soseki

Chapter 9
The Colour of Thoughts

"The soul becomes dyed with the colour of its thoughts." – **Marcus Aurelius**

Beyond the power of the biggest guns, the most explosive bombs, the most searing fires, and the most biting winds, there is something that can do more harm or more good than anything else. Powerful enough to make kings of ordinary men, and to undermine whole empires, words are all powerful. Words can rally troops, soothe broken hearts, inspire nations, and deceive, mislead and defraud entire populations.

Words are like water. While they feel soft to the touch, they can wear down mountain ranges and gouge canyons a mile deep into the landscape. But it is their gentleness that makes them so powerful. Governments with the biggest armies are so frightened of the power of words they will go to great lengths to silence them. Journalists disappear, writers are discredited, and the most eloquent orators are feared by the men in the ivory towers.

But words are so powerful they can convince us to give up our freedom of thought – our own capacity for decision-making – to those whose wordsmithery we find to be more powerful and compelling than our own. They convince us to buy things we don't need, believe ideas that aren't true, and cause harm to ourselves and others by distorting our view of reality so much we can no longer tell what's real and what's important any more. We are no longer able to determine what's right and what's wrong. We need guidebooks, bibles, religious texts and legalese to tell us how to behave because we trust those words more than we trust the words of common sense in our own heads. With words we can be convinced to value profits, pride, identity and hatred over humanity and empathy and kindness. Economics and material gain over our own welfare and the planet that gives us life.

"Only when the last tree has died and the last river been poisoned and the last fish been caught will we realise we cannot eat money," sates the Cree proverb.

The biggest atrocities in the human history were carried out by ordinary men who had been manipulated by the words of others. Suffering persists in all corners of the world because men believe the words, they are told more than the powerful intrinsic forces of love, compassion, unity and kindness. Empowered by words such as fear, profit, threat, danger, others, whole communities can be driven to evil.

If we use the right words, we can convince someone of anything. We can convince him that he's having the time of his life, even when his trousers are on fire. We can convince him to vote for the person who will do him the most harm. In the most eloquent words of Malcom X, people can be convinced into "hating the people who are being oppressed and loving the people who are doing the oppressing."

Words are can be powerful, life-changing and important – we can use their power to build and destroy entire worlds – yet all too often we throw them away as if they are worth nothing. Words are so powerful and wonderful, that if we choose them carefully selected words, we can show people that the sun is shining when all they can see are the holes in their shoes. We can show people their beauty, when all they see is judgement and criticism, and we can make people aware of the power, the unique skills and the untapped potential that they have within in them.

With the right words we can empower people to be and do better. We can show the worthless their worth. We can teach those who loathe themselves to love themselves. And we can share with the world the miracles and the magic that happen every day, in front of their faces, inches away, so close they can reach out and touch them, yet invisible to those who have been taught not to see them.

We so rarely harness this power to brighten anyone's day. Instead we choose to use it for darker purposes, because the gratification is quicker, though less nourishing. We use it to cast judgement on others, to create narratives that become self-fulfilling prophecies, convincing others that they and their world are pointless. We convince them that the hand they've been dealt is a weak one, and that this meagre lot is all they deserve. They simply aren't good enough to experience contentment, joy or happiness. But that's ok. There's only so much of that to go around anyway, and it's best not wasted on them.

We criticise and complain, our words bringing negative energy into our lives and the lives of those around us. We undermine others, and rather than using our words to build something wonderful we use them to destroy. It would be so easy to encourage, support, to celebrate, but instead we scoff, and snarl and humiliate. But instead we use them to put others down, to hold them back, lest our own lack of achievement be brought under scrutiny.

We moan and we whinge and we whine and the air is blue with our miserable nonsense. And then we wonder why the world has no good words for us.

Words have the power to start wars and kill whole generations, but they also have the power to unite entire peoples. Words can bring down walls, heal old wounds, and create lush landscapes for generations to come. And if we were to put aside our cowardice, fear and selfishness, step aside from our pride and our ego, we could all be so much wealthier and our world so much greener. The trees we plant today will offer shelter to those who need it tomorrow.

If we were to let go of our narrative of negativity, and start using words in a fertile, nourishing way, we could bring together an entire planet, united under a single cause. With words we could acknowledge our differences, embrace the things that make us unique, and work together to banish all the ills of this world, and turn it into a utopia, orbiting our golden sun as it nourishes crops, and warms us as we heal each other, as we cure diseases, as we put down our weapons and explore the stars, as we build the bravest future anyone could imagine.

But there are other words that prevent us from doing such positive work. The words of conflict and competition, spoken by all among us, but mostly by our stunted leaders, serve not to see mankind thrive, but to see small portions of mankind perform marginally better, often at the expense of the others. The words of the elite classes scupper true progress by attaching greater value to dated notions of tribalism, which should have been buried with the emperors in the pyramids of Egypt, but which instead prevail in our government buildings and in our boardrooms.

And driving all of this are the words we speak to ourselves. The limiting, suffocating self-talk of fear and ego and pride.

Deep inside ourselves there is a narrative taking place that has a stranglehold on our identity – our sense of self. It distorts the world around us, and impacts the quality of life we can ever expect to have. The words we are using to speak to ourselves today are defining what our life will be like tomorrow, next year, in ten years' time. The words we use to talk to ourselves, focusing our attention on our anxieties, our blunders and disappointments, our weaknesses, our excuses and inabilities, these words are setting the scene for the life we are living in the real world. They are setting us up to live in a world of hostility, where the risk is too great, where it's every person for themselves, where danger lurks around every corner.

Like a genie granting wishes, if you think you're not good enough, then this will be the truth that you will speak to yourself, and it will become manifest in your life. If you think you're worthless, then worthless you will be. If you despise yourself, loathe yourself, undermine yourself, talk to yourself like you talk about others, then you sabotage any chance you have of creating a life you truly deserve and realising your potential. If you use your words to invite negativity into your life, then your life will become negative.

You sabotage your opportunity to create a better world for yourself and for others.

When your internal voice tells you that you'll fail, you're unlikely to try. When your internal narrative is filled with stories about every time you've fallen down, chances are you won't try to get up. If you use words to keep others down, how can you use words to lift yourself up?

The way we talk about the world around us describes exactly the world we see within us. When we see danger, obstacles and ugliness, we are describing our own fears, insecurities and negative inner dialogue. When we relish the opportunity to criticise, to judge, to undermine the confidence of others, we are speaking volumes about ourselves. Our harshness, cruelty and aggression reveal our weakness, self-doubt and insecurity.

But words can paint a picture of a different kind. Words can describe a blossoming garden, can summon a supernova that lights up a galaxy, or tell us about the individual strands of silk in the finest of robes. And when you harness this power over your internal narrative, you can speak energy into your identity from the inside out. Just as words can be used to manipulate good men to commit atrocities, you can use words to rebuild yourself not as someone who is weak, a failure, gripped with anxiety, but as someone who has strength, compassion, who learns from mistakes and understands that failure is a part of success. You can begin to describe yourself as someone who has the power to help others, to achieve great things, who doesn't see success and joy and contentment as abstract concepts reserved for others, but can imagine them happening for real.

By rewording our internal dialogue, we can start to describe ourselves in terms of our strengths, the things that make us unique, our abilities and our victories, and the offering we can bring to the world that no other human can. We can begin to see our worth, we can refuse to be damaged by the negative words of others but choose to own the words that shape and describe our world.

These words are ours, and we can wield them as instruments of creation, to create the world we want for ourselves, the world we want for others, and to be the kind of person we have always wanted to be.

It's my snow, I think,
And the weight on my hat
Lightens

-    Takarai Kikaku

Chapter 10
Lightness of Presence

"A bird sings that only you can hear." – Jack Kornfield

So concerned are we about the past, or so afraid of the future, that we rarely spend time in the present. Yet, that's where we find ourselves, continually, from the moment we're born to the moment we move on to the next thing. So attached are we to things that have either gone and are no more or things that have yet to occur, that we put no effort into being present for the things that actually are.

But that's where everything is.

Everything exists right now. It is the only thing that can be, with any sense, considered real. Those things that have already happened are now long gone, just ghosts that haunt our consciousness, while those things that have yet to take place are figments of our imagination. That is, until they happen, at which time they will no longer be the future, but will instead transition quickly into being in the past. They will exist for just a fleeting moment and, in all likelihood, we will probably be either too concerned with something that has either occurred beforehand or that may or may not be due to occur sometime afterwards, to really notice at all.
Blink and you'll miss it.

But here, right now, is where everything is, and unless we pay attention, it will have passed without so much as a by your leave. Yet when we do pay attention – with intention – our awareness unfurls before us like a blossoming lotus flower. And as its petals unwrap themselves in the sunshine and its fragrance fills the air, our worries about the past and our anxiety about the future drift away, and we find ourselves here. Right here. Present. Correct. Immaculate. Divine.

When we stop everything and become aware, we are able to step aside from everything that clouds our view and recognise those things that have such a huge influence over us that we spend most of our time believing that they are us. But they are not.

Suddenly those silly things we invested so much emotional energy in turn to trifles, then to dust, and then they blow away on the breeze that soothes us, and we find ourselves. Revealed.

In the same way that the hats we wear on our heads and the coats we wear on our backs aren't parts of our anatomy, so too are our fears, biases, prejudices and self-defeating thoughts and attitudes. And though, just like clothes they appear as part of our identity, they aren't truly a part of our real, authentic self. And in this recognition of these adornments, they too can turn to dust and blow away, leaving us behind, our eyes open.

With this new clarity the light pours in, and through the lens of awareness we are free to explore ourselves and the universe that stretches out from us in every direction. We become aware of textures, smells and tastes. We become aware of the inner processes of our ego that our true selves hide behind. We become aware of time and our place in it. And suddenly we can really feel what it is to exist and to be, and we are energised to explore, to do and to love.

When we stretch out our arms at our sides, and reach with our fingers, we feel every sinew in our torso as they release the tensions that have built up throughout the day. And just as a newborn stretches after a lengthy sleep, in that moment our worries disappear as we connect with the sensations of our bodies.

As we walk through the world with our eyes open, we become aware of the experiences of colour, of the feeling of air, of temperature and taste and sound. We are connected to everything, and everything opens up before us, like the layers of an onion. And we are invited to delve deeper and deeper into everything around us, the sensations and our ability to recognise and appreciate them becomes heightened, more sensitive, and more powerful.

The more we experience the world around us, the more we experience ourselves, becoming fluent with awareness, and the experiences we are exploring here and now. Where we end and the world begins becomes vague as we see everything with crystal clarity. We are connected. Entwined. Contiguous and continuous.

This new awareness, this connection we have with this moment, this sea of sensation that we find ourselves in is worlds apart from where we were a moment ago. Yet this is the same road we've always walked down, the same streets and the same houses. As we have changed and shed the burdens of yesterday and tomorrow, the universe has risen up to meet us.

When we are able to cleanse ourselves of the reality distorting influences of ego, of bias, of our own notion of Identity and who we're supposed to be, and withdraw ourselves from the past and the future, we are able to use our own awareness as a magnifying glass to see everything in immaculate detail. By focusing on the beauty of the world, our world becomes more beautiful, and as soon as we recognise this, we begin to recognise that we have the power to shape our lives, to bend reality to our own will. Beauty springs up wherever we cast our gaze. And it is so detailed it takes our breath away.

Instead of allowing life to weigh down on us like an incredible burden, we can instead choose to pick it up and play with it, dance with it, and shape it in our hands like an artist sculpting a piece of clay. We can choose to find the light on the darkest days, to find the magic in poetry, the opportunity in the challenges, and the music in the buzzing of the bees. Thunderstorms become percussive accompaniment to the opera of our day. Traffic jams become escapes from our hardships. Strangers become friends we haven't met yet.

We can offer hope to the hopeless, lend a hand to those struggling on the steps, and give an ear to those who feel unheard. We can share the beauty we see around us and offer the vista to others to enjoy.

In this moment the sound of the wind in the trees becomes a symphony that celebrates life, and even the muddiest puddles reflect back the most beautiful skies. Here in the moment we have the opportunity to really touch the infinite universe that we find ourselves at the centre of, which stretches out from us in all directions, and to choose what to do with this immense freedom.

In this moment we are unable to hold on to hate or anger. In this moment we have no choice but to let go and surrender to the time and place we find ourselves in. And in this letting go we forgive everyone, love everyone, and as our muscles relax and calm descends, we find joy and loving awareness creeping in to fill the void.

In this moment, there is only love. Everything we touch, everything we feel, everything that we are aware of offers new insights and experiences. Opportunities to understand and to share. Opportunities to finally know what it is to simply be.

We are here. In this moment. That is the only truth. And that give us the power and the freedom to see and do and be whatever we want to be. And it gives us the freedom to be only good energy, good light, and to tread gently. It makes us immortal and infinite. We are compassionate and understanding, we are patient and connected, we are free to see the pain and suffering in ourselves and everyone around us. To acknowledge it, thank it for all it has taught us, and then to send it on its way, with a breath and a smile.

We are free to let go.

With this release we find ourselves wanting for nothing and blessed with all we could ever possibly need. We shed our fear and in doing so the universe reflects back an image of ourselves that is generous and smiles kindly upon us. Roads lead in all directions, and all lead to prosperity and contentment. We can choose to walk any path, or we can choose to stay right here – just as long as we choose.

Fearless, we can be anything we want. Fearless, we can go anywhere, do anything, understand who we are, tackle any obstacle, climb any mountain. In this new moment of clarity, with ego and pride left at the door, we see what we need to do, what we are prepared to do, and what obstacles we need to overcome. We see ourselves, and as we grow younger the worry lines disappear. We see our shoulders relax and our back straighten. We see the skin tighten and the muscles grow strong. We see ourselves, confident, capable, calm.

We are unintimidated, we are in a position of strength and power that transcends any conflict or fight. We are here, and from here we can go anywhere. We are ready to make the decision.

But just for this moment we will leave that decision for the future. Because right now we're happy in this moment, listening to the birdsong and the wind in the leaves, basking in the golden sun, recharging our batteries like a butterfly warming its wings, letting go of everything that hurts us, appreciating where we are, who we are, and all that surrounds us. Right now, we are connected by our ethereal threads to everything that has ever been or will ever be, every person, every moment, every thought, idea or feeling.

And those threads are humming like aeolian harps, lulling us into a comfortable embrace of connectedness, and everything becomes light.

Life is beautiful if you know how to look at it.

In a world
Of grief and pain,
Flowers bloom –
Even then.

– Kobayashi Issa

Chapter 11
A Matter of Identity

"Identity is an assemblage of constellations." – **Anna Deavere Smith**

When we find ourselves alone with our awareness, maybe in a quiet time of reflection, during meditation or out in nature, we become an observer not just of the infinite, but our part in it, and our part as it. We become infinite just as the wave is the sea and the raindrop is the ocean.

And as an observer we are also aware of our disconnectedness. We are able to witness things as separate from ourselves. We are not our bodies – our arms and legs – just as we are not the clothes we wear. Yet often we identify with both our clothes and our physical forms. We have 'our style' and associate with the way we dress, just as we associate with the person in the mirror.

But alone with our awareness we become an observer of these things, and as much as they are a part of us, we can choose to observe them separately just as we observe the ground we walk as being separate from us, the fragrance of the flowers as we brush past them, the person sat opposite us on the train, the birds in the sky.

Just as we are connected to these things, these people, these places and these ideas in our infinite continuum of being, so too are we able to align with our awareness to observe them as an objective witness. And just as we are able to observe our hands and our feet and our physical presence as being distinct from us, so to can we become distinctly separate observers of the processes that go on inside us.

Through the practice of meditation, we can tune our focus into our breathing or a mantra or another single point, and from there observe our thoughts as they pass us by. Through practice we can choose to give strength to those thoughts that serve us, and take power away from those thoughts which serve to undermine us. We can work to take away the power that is exerted upon us by anxiety, overcome our depression, and let go of the ghosts of the past so that we can build a brighter future for ourselves and those around us by focusing our energy onto the present moment.

And just as we are able to focus awareness onto our thoughts and emotional traits and choose to distance ourselves from those that we no longer wish to control us, we can also focus on ourselves. With self-awareness we can isolate our anger, our negative characteristics, our self-defeating habits and patterns by choosing to disassociate ourselves from them.

Once we were highly strung with a short fuse, but now we have allowed those traits to disappear and we are calm and unflappable. Where we were selfish, we are now compassionate. Where we had no time for others, now we actively listen. Where we were flawed, we give ourselves time to heal our wounds.

When we allow our ego and our pride to evaporate, we can see ourselves in all our broken glory, and honestly admit where the cracks are, instead of defensively claiming there are none. Where we would rather engage in conflict to simply prove our point and save face, we are happy to now choose our battles in the interests of peace. Where once we would rush to get there first, we now enjoy the luxury of a more pedestrian journey and arrive soon after, calm and serene.

Alone with our awareness we can see how the traumas of the past have shaped us and continue to traumatise us through our identity. But now we can let it go, and the people who hurt us, and the things we did to ourselves, they no longer have a grip on us, and we can get back to the important business of being ourselves. After all, what is forgiveness if not letting go?

As we watch all the trappings of the past, all our negative traits, all the things that hurt, that hold us back, that cripple us and fill us with sorrow and fear drift away, we find ourselves lighter now that we are not burdened with all the trappings of pride and ego. We are no longer the angry guy, the bitter guy, the opinionated guy, the victim. We are no longer the guy who is incapable, who would never do that, who is afraid, who can't. We are no longer so possessed by pride and ego that we pretend we aren't broken, and let that internal pain dominate our identity.

Now that we are not holding ourselves back, finding reasons not to do things, try things and take risks – "people like me don't do things like that" – we feel empowered, and anything is possible. We embark on mini adventures that grow into triumphs and epic tales of empire building and success.

But there is a question that lingers.

All those things – the things that weighed us down, stopped us from moving forward, tortured us, defined us, were part of our identity. They were the things that we clung on to, that gave us a sense of self. But now we have disassociated ourselves from them.

Now that we are alone with our awareness, and we are observing these things – these former parts of us which now lie discarded like a pile of dirty clothes in the corner of the room, who are we?

If we are not our anxiety, our inability to get things done, the victim of bad luck and tragedy, the failure, the idiot, the thug or the angry man, what remains? If we are no longer the person who can't, the indecisive man, the sad case, the forlorn, the lost, the lonely and the sorrowful, who are we?

Like a snake that sheds its dead skin we find ourselves reborn, revealed at last into the light, filled with the energy of potential. Alone with our awareness and our new skin we find we are perfectly placed to rebuild ourselves with things that remain. To recapture the wonder of the world around us, to let go of the things that cloud our view and really look, with new eyes, at the opportunity and the potential and the abundance of the world around us.

Now that we have released our anxiety and the fears that are holding us back, we feel ready to leap with the energy of a coiled spring, into an exciting new unknown. We want to dance and sing and celebrate because... why not?

It doesn't matter what anyone else thinks because it's not about them and it's not for them. No longer do you need anyone else's approval or permission, because you have the power to grant it to yourself. The old you lived a life defined by others. A life defined by the things that happened to you, by the things that were said to you, by the things that you did to yourself and by the standards and values of others.

The old you lived a life that was inauthentic. Doing what you thought a person like you should do, instead of what an uninhibited version of yourself could do, you tried to please everyone else, or fit into a pigeon hole, or a groove created by those who went before, or by convention. The old you was limited by imaginary rules, by hypothetical boundaries that didn't exist, scared of what might go wrong. Carrying the burden of the past and terrified of the future.

But the new you is unlimited. Excited by what might go right, the world sparkles with opportunities yet to be embraced. Uninhibited by anything that went before, you now see your power, you can feel the vibration of your ethereal threads connecting you with an unlimited, infinite expanse of ideas, opportunity, visions and dreams.

Anything is possible if you rise to the challenge. You can be whoever you want to be as long as you're prepared to let go of who you think you are and who you were. Each night we die and each morning we are born again, as sure as the sun follows the moon. And tomorrow brings with it a new chance at life.

Alone with our awareness we give thanks to the lessons of the past and acknowledge the role that they've played in getting us this far. But this life is ours, and unless we live it as ourselves – our authentic, unburdened selves – we will never enjoy the life we are due and the life we deserve.

It is there, like an echo, waiting for us to tune in. We need to turn down the background noise, let go of the voices of anxiety, which serve to distract us from our own message, our own calling. And as we step aside and align with our awareness the paralysing voices within get quieter, and our calling gets louder.

Stop for a moment and listen. Let go of everything and just listen. Release your authentic self from its burdens and live your authentic life. You are reborn each day, and each day is your day to shine.

Life,
Is like a butterfly,
Whatever it is.

– Nishiyamo Sōin

Chapter 12
Choose Your Inputs

"But what good is the popular opinion, if the lot of us just process like minions?" – **Criss Jami**

We're being hacked. Right now, there are entities around us attempting to hack us, attempting to change our thoughts, our beliefs, our bodies and our behaviours. I'm even trying to do it to you with the words in this book.

Wherever we turn there are parties attempting to influence us and control us by introducing us to ideas, images, notions, concepts and products that are designed to make us act, feel and think in a particular way. Politicians, news media, brands all want to bend us to their will. They want us to buy their goods and services, vote for and legitimise their politics, validate their notion of what's good and bad and moral and right. Or they just encourage us to behave in a way that works for them. And to do this they are hacking us.

Of course, some degree of manipulation is useful in day to day life. We have been hacked so that we follow certain shared behaviours that benefit everyone. We all agree to stop our vehicles at red lights, for example, and despite there being no physical barrier to prevent us progressing forward when a red light is showing, most of us would find it very difficult to break this programming.

Indeed, we have our values and beliefs manipulated all the time. There was a time when driving home after a few drinks at the pub was normal behaviour, these days it is commonly accepted that climbing into your car after even one or two drinks is shameful. We are encouraged to make other behaviours habitual parts of our routine – regular exercise and drinking plenty of water is not only good for us, but it's good for the system too. Healthy workers are more productive and are less of a strain on the medical infrastructure.

Publicity campaigns to control the spread of flu and other illnesses have been hugely beneficial, and today there are agencies dedicated to creating and manipulating human behaviour. Disciplines within architecture are dedicated to designing buildings and public spaces that guide and control human movements. Millions are spent on the study of human behavioural patterns and how to influence them. The placement of the 'buy it now' button on the web page. The lines painted on the supermarket floor. The classical music played over the loudspeakers at the bus station. The design of arm rests on park benches. All efforts to promote some behaviours and reduce others.

Sometimes it's for our benefit, so that we don't get hit by falling masonry, or bitten by the monkeys at the safari park. Other times it's to make us feel as if we're in control – not all buttons at pedestrian crossings actually do anything. But other times it's less than beneficial.

Big corporations want us to buy their products, so that the CEO can afford his private island and the shareholders get their cut. So, they spend billions on carefully constructed advertising campaigns designed to connect with us on an emotional level. Other times they simply instruct us what to do, and we can't resist. Drink Coke.

But other times they want to manipulate our belief systems, in order to keep us under control, subservient and serving their own cause – or at least not threatening it. They aim to use information to keep us divided, to keep us placid, docile and afraid of what lurks... out there.

"The meek shall inherit the earth," they tell us. Meek people are quiet and timid. Meek people do what they're told. Meek people don't cause any trouble.

Those people who are fleeing their own country because their own leaders are dropping bombs on them – bombs that we've sold them – are a threat to us. They're criminals and rapists, and most definitely not people just like us, under extraordinary pressure and in need of help. People like you and me, desperate for the outstretched hand of hope and humanity.

No, those people, who have travelled for months with all their possessions on their backs are a danger, a threat, and we must be afraid. The world is a dangerous place, the streets aren't safe, and are filled with people who look different, speak a different language, and are therefore a threat. We should fear them, despise them, hate them. Stay indoors where its safe. Consume more media, more products, feed the system and don't challenge the status quo.

There is much to be afraid of. Our food is out to kill us. The earth is toxic. Any fruit or vegetable that doesn't meet the same standards of cleanliness and uniformity that we buy at the supermarket must be viewed with suspicion. Don't grow your own, those carrots look different. Better to eat cheap, mass produced, heavily processed food instead.

Consume, be afraid, be disgusted, do as you're told, think as you're meant to think. As long as the flow of information into your mind is controlled by another, you are being hacked. As long as the food you eat is being controlled by another, you are being hacked.

Tobacco, alcohol, sugar, news, outrage, fear, anger, gossip, all serves to control and distract. How many of your opinions have been arrived at independently, and how much of it is based on inputs that are designed to cause a reaction? How much of the news you read is designed to make you angry? To pit you against another group of humans?

How many of your choices – what you eat, who you vote for, who you avoid in a crowded place – are influenced by those who control the means of production? How much of what you consume – both physically and mentally – is carefully curated by editors and buyers? Did you even realise the last time you subconsciously obeyed a call to action?

How much of your behaviour and beliefs serve those who benefit from keeping us apart, siloed, afraid of the unknown and the different? Who benefits from us being consumers of not just their goods, but also their ideas, and their propaganda? Whose arms deals, exploitation of overseas labour and tax havens, pillaging of the environment goes unchallenged because they've distracted us with other concerns to occupy us, other morsels to gorge ourselves on, other toxic ideas to keep us looking the other way?

How much of what you buy is influenced by advertising? Do you even realise that you're being advertised at all the time? How much of your behaviour and thought processes are actually your own? What about your values? What if you were to start thinking for yourself, on behalf of yourself? What would the world look like then?

Would you be able to see yourself in those who have crossed the unforgiving seas in search of safety and hope? Where previously there had been fear would you be able to finder wonder, opportunity and love? When you reject the ready meals in favour of the home-cooked and the home grown, will you be amazed by a new universe of flavour? When you reject the pre-digested thoughts of those who benefit from your outrage, are you free to create more beautiful, poetic thoughts for yourself?

When you stop being guided by others towards someone you can blame, where do you find yourself?

When we choose our inputs instead of having them chosen for us, we can build a world that serves us, that offers us a kaleidoscope of joy and colour. When we are no longer consumers who, like dairy cattle eating our fill from the trough while oblivious that we're being milked, but are instead producers of art, of poetry, and ideas, our worlds become much more interesting. More vibrant. More alive.

When we learn that fear gets in the way of collaboration and choose to break down barriers instead of hiding behind them, to work with our colleagues 'over there' instead of being terrified of them, maybe we will see just how far humanity can go. But when we cower behind outrage and disgust, we are going nowhere.

When we can choose our own inputs, we are free to choose a world view free of conflict. A world view where profit doesn't come from human suffering and the mass market, but from the creation of great things. New achievements can be realised. Mankind can reach for the stars.

When we turn off our televisions, turn our back on the billboards, put down our smartphones and look up from the feeding troughs, suddenly colours become more vivid. The dance of the bees on the cherry blossom becomes entrancing. Sounds become music, the air we breathe revitalises and energises us, and dew drops reveal new ways of seeing.

When we stop comparing our lives with the lives of the pretend people in the television commercials, with their nice clothes and amazing teeth, we realise that we're wealthier than we ever thought. There is no need that cannot be sated by a walk in the evening sunlight, by the feeling of a cool breeze on your face, or the sound of the waves caressing the shore.

Here in this moment, when we resist the propaganda and stop ourselves being distracted by the flashing lights and the catchy slogans, we find ourselves suddenly free, and the entire universe offers itself up to us. We can go anywhere, do anything, be anyone. We are no longer being led, but we are driven, and ahead of us lies the road of our choosing. And it's up to us now which journey we undertake.

Do we choose the path of opportunity, of compassion and empathy, of unity and dreams? Or do we choose the path of hostility, of fear, of closed doors, greed and selfishness? When we get to choose our own inputs, are we more likely to choose those which hurt us or those which bring us joy?

When we find ourselves in a world filled with love and kindness and compassion, are we more likely to let that infect our being and spread like wild flowers? Or are we likely to turn our backs on everything this world has to offer, to turn our backs on unlimited abundance, and instead choose to close our doors and grip tightly to the meagre riches that we have right here, and right now?

When we fill our hearts and our minds with stories of hope, with ideas for growth and benefit, do we find ourselves filled with the urge to make the world a better place? And do we adopt actions and behaviours that create, that nurture, that benefit others as much as they benefit us? Or do we destroy with pessimism and bile?

By choosing our inputs we have the opportunity to manipulate our own beliefs and behaviours, to undertake not to be controlled by external forces for their benefit, but to take action for our benefit and the benefit of others. By choosing our own inputs we can create a world that is alive with meaning, with music, colour and texture. Or we can be fed our inputs by those who profit from our fear, and find ourselves poisoned by processed food, hiding indoors from the dangers outside, afraid of everyone and anyone who looks different or sounds different. Subservient, terrified, caged and alone. Angry.

The world is a buffet – a pick-and-mix of joy and hate, of fear and love, of abundance and scarcity, of freedom and confinement. We can choose whichever we want, and the choice is ours. But if we hand over that choice to those who benefit from our fear and dissatisfaction, our worlds grow smaller, the skies grow greyer, and our opportunities for joy grow fewer.

Rather than being fed at the silage trough like cattle, we can choose to feed ourselves from the broadest, most varied menu we can imagine. All that's required is that we make the choice to do so. All we have to do is take decisive action. We may find that some things are off the menu, but whatever we end up with will be infinitely more nourishing than the fodder at the trough. We may even have to go foraging and hunting for ourselves if we really wish to have the finest meals, and some days we will go hungry, but the hardship will have been worth it to really live, and live a life less ordinary.

When we nourish ourselves by choosing our own inputs, we finally get to see who we really are. For so long we've been hacked and manipulated, and like puppets on string our actions have been the intent of others rather than the intent of our own. But now we see who we really are, and we can be proud to have uncovered our own philosophy, our own motivations, and our own values. We don't need to be told the difference between right and wrong by a religious text, because we can tell the difference for ourselves. We don't need to be told how to behave by the rule of law because we know the difference between good and evil. And we see that those who created those rules in the first place did so not because they thought this was where righteousness lay, but because they need us to do as we're told so they could go about their own business.

It's time now for us to go about our business. It's time for us to cut the cord that ties us to the ideologies of others, and forge a path of kindness, of positive energy, that will lead us where we need to go. And in doing so we will shine a light so that others' routes may also be illuminated.

Living our life means making our choices and not having them made for us. We already have everything we need. It's time to move forward.

Even after waking
From the dream
I'll see the colours of irises.

—   Ogawa Shūshik

Chapter 13
About Them

"You're not free in life until you're free of wanting other people's approval." – **Dawn Steel**

There is a book which claims to tell us what's right and what's wrong. There are legal documents in an archive, which set out the correct way to behave in society. There are magazines that make examples of anybody who dares not conform or fit in to prescribed notions of beauty or celebrity. And there are armies of people, millions of them, all waiting to take a shot at anybody who puts their head above the parapet by embracing their uniqueness or by being different. At anyone being themselves.

Too fat. Too thin. Too gay. Too straight. Too foreign. Too unusual. Too difficult to categorise.

Fit in, we are told, wear the uniform, sing the anthem, wave the flag, and follow the rules. But heaven forbid you create your own value judgements. No, we must deny our humanity and become one of the crowd. There is, after all, safety in numbers. And standing out, shining, creating our art, deciding our own future distinct from the one that has already been decided for us – and for people like us – is dangerous.

Dangerous for us. Dangerous for the shared consensus of what is normal.

If we shrink into the background, do what we're told, with the permission and validation of the rule makers, then we might just make it through the day unscathed. We might avoid the harsh words, and the ridicule, and the rolling eyeballs and the gossip. And then when we wake up again tomorrow to face the same gauntlet, we can try again to not be noticed, to keep our heads down, to not rock the boat, and to safely disappear.

And this approach of the surface world with its shallow rewards, has worked for whole generations, and it still works for some today. Once upon a time a job for life and toeing the line resulted in slow and steady growth, and in retirement the rewards would come, the mortgage would be paid off, the children will have flown the nest and finally we can enjoy the savings, the wine from the cellar, and possibly a walk to the end of the garden, should our creaking joints allow it.

But that reward is a carrot dangling from a stick, just out of reach. There are no more jobs for life, there is no more slow and steady growth, and retirement gets further and further away. Fitting in, disappearing into the crowd, becoming faceless, nameless, and denying our unique humanity no longer delivers the rewards that we were led to believe would be waiting for us.

It's time to explore a different path.

Only, this new path is filled with risk. On this path we no longer have the permission of others, or the validation of the tried and the trusted. When we step out from the flock we become prey for the wolves yet, strangely, we're more afraid of the sheep. Exposed, we fear the judgement of those who find security in the group, and who disapprove of those who seek to go their own way. Stepping away from the road well-travelled means running the gauntlet, braving the harsh words, and the ridicule, and the rolling eyeballs and the gossip. These things are the price to be paid for celebrating our uniqueness and realising our true selves.

In the past we would seek the permission of the crowd, of those close to us, those whose opinion we value and those we raise up on pedestals because we believe they are the ones who know the path and where they're going. But all along they've just been following the paths of others, and now the weeds are starting to take over.

When we realise that nobody really knows the best path to take, we become just like the American explorers Lewis and Clark of the 1800s, navigating our own way through this unknown and treacherous land. Cutting back the vines that obstruct us, forging ahead, we must become deaf to the warnings of those less brave, to the criticisms of those who call us foolish for trying. We become deaf to the protestations and the ridicule of those who want us to be boring so that they don't have to be interesting.

In the past we would be paralysed, unable to make decisions, deferring instead to those upon whose mighty shoulders we could ride. But those shoulders grew weary with the responsibility of being our wayfarers, and now we must empower ourselves to make our own choices, plot a course – any course – because drifting on the rafts of others has led us to where we are today. Lost at sea. And it's time to swim for shore.

Becoming decisive means facing the consequences of those decisions, but it is the most powerful thing we can do. Sometimes that can mean making decisions that will change our lives dramatically, sometimes it means making decisions that will change the world. Other times it means deciding to do nothing at all. But always, we must empower ourselves to make decisions or have no power over our lives.

And all of this must be done with our own approval. If we wait for the blessing of others we will wait forever and all the while we'll be handing over the steering to those who don't know where we need to go, only where they think we need to go. Ultimately, that will leave us lost. Instead we must decide for ourselves where we need to go and steer ourselves in that direction – and often we won't even know what that direction is until we get there and find ourselves en-route to a new tomorrow, different to today.

And the eyes will roll, and the criticisms will come. But what you're doing, you're not doing for them. You are doing these things for yourself, and along the way you will find your cheerleaders – some will have always been there and new supporters will join them – and they will celebrate your decisions. With their support you will get stronger, and the dissenting voices behind you will get quieter and more distant. And you will find strength knowing that you took this course and it is yours alone.

When we hand over decision making to others, we become beholden to them. Not only does this burden them, but it weakens us. We find ourselves eager not to upset anyone, yet we feel responsible for those who will be upset anyway. In attempting to keep everyone around us happy we ultimately become unhappy ourselves, and in the process we fail in our mission to please everyone else. Only when we find our own happiness can we share it with others, and even if it doesn't resonate with everyone, we find the power to shrug off the emotional states that don't serve us or aren't about us.

As long as we have stepped forward with gentle loving kindness, and as long as we have sought to use our light to brighten the paths of others, we cannot be responsible for those who wish to remain in the darkness. They will find their own way, or they will not, but when their day comes you can be their cheerleader and support them on their journey. You can shine a light on their path to help them on their journey. But they have to walk it.

So, for now, let go of the happiness of others, and you will find their happiness increases. Let go of your own desires and you will find your desires fulfilled. Stop searching, stop focusing on what you don't have, and relish everything you do have. When you attempt to please everyone you will please no one, but when you focus on your own radiating happiness, it will spread contagiously and vibrantly, spreading outwards like a golden sunrise.

Those who scoff – you're not doing it for them. Those who deride and critique – they're not your audience. Even if it's just an audience of one, remaining close to your convictions will bring its own rewards.

The approval and validation of others requires a watering down of your authenticity and your power. It requires that you lose a sense of yourself. When you are emotionally dependent on the actions of others, on the emotional wellbeing of others, you cause yourself pain as you yearn for their approval in order that you may feel worthy. But this drains and weakens all parties – especially you – and relationships begin to crack and break down, taking your self-esteem with them.

When you take responsibility for your own emotional wellbeing, when you become emotionally independent, just as is the responsibility of every grown person who wishes to flourish, then you will radiate positivity, and others can choose to bask in that warmth. When you are filled with a good energy of your own, rather than needing to absorb the energy of others you become a beacon that attracts others who wish to enjoy your light.

By breaking free of a dependence on others and finding your inner strength, you will attract others to you. By not concerning yourself with their judgement, you will attract their positivity. Paradoxically, by not seeking the approval and validation of others, you will receive their validation and approval.

Do it for yourself, give yourself permission, and your strength will become magnetic.

Light of the moon
Moves west – flowers' shadows
Creep eastward

-    Yosa Buson

Chapter 14
About You

"Love is given, not received." – Naval Ravikant

The whole thing works because energy moves from one place to another. The whole, infinite, incomprehensible thing, is just a swirling maelstrom of energy moving from one place to another, from one form to another. Never destroyed, simply changing shape, purpose, transferred through processes, which themselves are created by the transfer of energy.

In the heart of the sun, atoms of hydrogen are fused together under great pressure and intense heat. In turn they release their energy and are transformed into helium atoms, and the sun continues to burn blindingly bright at the heart of our solar system, all of which is entrapped by its gravity, revolving around it in a majestic planetary dance of energy.

Eight and a half minutes and one astronomical unit later, the sun's energy reaches our blue and green marble, and the chlorophyll inside the leaves of plants converts the sun's light into energy. The plants can grow bigger, stronger, and bear fruit for animals – and for us – to eat.

As we chew, digest and break down the plant's generous fruit into its individual molecules, the mitochondria in our cells convert them into energy. This energy drives the movement of our muscles and keeps our metabolism running, so that we can breathe, love, skip, sing, and take part in this whole beautiful ballet.

And in every action we perform, every movement we make, every breath we inhale, the energy is transferred and transformed again and again. It becomes sound energy as we speak and tap our feet on the floor. It becomes motion as we move, and it becomes heat as our bodies regulate their temperature automatically. And as the energy leaves us and carries on its journey, it becomes obvious that the transfer of energy is not just how we stay alive, but it is life itself. Without it, nothing would move, and everything would be dark and cold.

In every action throughout the universe, there is this transfer of energy. Subatomic particles shake and quake with energy, and even in the darkest, coldest reaches of the universe where those vibrations are much slower, they still persist despite being near absolute zero. And energy is, as always, transferred.

Energy exists in ideas too. Thoughts generated in our minds by the transfer of electrochemical energy along our neurones and across our synapses have their own frequency, their own energy. When the energy of our thoughts, actions, and ideas resonates at a high frequency, our positivity radiates outwards, and our abundant energy is transferred to the world around us. But when our energy is negative and weak, we absorb the energy that is radiated by others, leaving them weakened and drained.

In this way the energy of our actions can raise up, or it can bring down. We can use our energy to create, to do good, to share love and to change the world. Or we can use it to spread fear and negativity, destructive ideas and philosophies. Our energy can build walls to keep people frightened, caged and apart, or it can bring people together to further the human spirit. It can crush people's dreams, or it can offer encouragement and support. It can bring us, and those around us, closer to rock bottom and defeat, or it can help people to grow and thrive, just like the light that takes eight-and-a-half minutes to reach the green leaves on Earth.

Every day we are faced with opportunities to use our energy for good, to help others, and to extend helping hands to those who might need them. Those hands may be sharing food with someone who finds themselves hungry, they may applaud someone who is embarking on a new adventure, or they may lay the foundations for the creation of something new. Those hands may guide someone who's lost, or they might offer comfort and support to someone who is having a bad day, or wave to a departing loved one to let them know they'll be missed.

The same hands that throw punches and stones, could just as easily plant seeds of encouragement, or cradle a child who won't settle. The hands that build barriers between peoples could just as easily tear those barriers down. The hands that hold daggers could instead stitch up wounds.

The same energy to destroy can be used to build.

Every day we are faced with the chance to raise our vibration. Do we laugh and point at the person who falls on their face, or do we bend down to help them up? Do we give our spare coins as alms to the needy, or do we fritter them away? Is our vibration high and resonating at a positive frequency, or is it low and negative? What is our default vibration and how do we raise it?

When someone gets in our way on the street, is our initial reaction to tut in annoyance, or to step back and allow them to pass? Are we the first to offer an apology and a helping hand, or do we find our defences raised before we have had a chance to assess the situation? In any given moment is our intent based on what is best for us, what is best for others, or what is best for all?

Raising our vibrations is not about being submissive to the wider world, but about recognising the needs of others, assuming positive intent before bad, and taking a moment to interrupt our negative patterns and train ourselves into new, beneficial ones. We will still get where we need to be going, we will still achieve what we need to achieve, but we will do it with the grace of a dancer instead of the brutality of a wrestler. Positivity allows us to skip through our days lightly leaving echoes of goodness behind, rather than slogging through them heavily and wearily leaving a trail of despair and destruction.

When we find our lives filled with abundant joy, do we seek to see how we can share it with others, or do we seek to protect our hard-fought winnings from those who would wish to steal them from us. Do we see a world of risk or a world of opportunity? When we wake

164

in the morning, do we prepare to do battle, or prepare to go in peace?

A default, resting state of negativity and conflict aligns us with a low frequency. And as vibrations harmonise, we will find ourselves resonating with the low energy of the world we move around in. Our low frequency will spread to others, and will draw negativity towards us. When someone gets in our way and we tut angrily, we find they react negatively, mirroring our negativity. Ever wonder why some people always seem to fall into trouble, while others don't? Ever wonder why some people have lives of drama, while others do not? Ever notice that those who complain the most have the most to complain about?

But it works the other way too. If we make every effort to raise our vibration, then we align ourselves with similarly positive energies around us. We find ourselves making new friends, surrounded by beauty and opportunity, and enjoying a life of colour and texture, even on the rainiest days. And what's more, simply by tuning ourselves into a higher frequency where we recognise beauty, giving others the help of the space that they need or by sharing our abundance, we play a small part in raising the collective vibration of humanity, and making our world, our universe, and the infinite continuum of being a better place.

Vibrations harmonise. Even the smallest positive vibration – the smallest positive act or thought – combines with the surrounding vibrations to grow bigger and stronger.

We see this manifest everywhere around us. When the collective energy of a people goes up, the nation prospers. Public health and wellbeing increase, unemployment falls, the infrastructure grows strong, and the underlying tone of the nation is happy. And it ripples outwards, as relationships with other nations grow stronger, trade improves - as do the respective economies, welfare and standards of living increase across the board. Wars become less frequent, disease and poverty decrease, and humanitarian and refugee crises become fewer.

But it can swing the other way too. When those with negative energy shout loud and long enough, the collective energy is brought down as it harmonises with those who wish to spread fear and discontent and anger and hatred. Public opinion shifts to the right, divisions increase, the politics of hostility prevails, and before long the state of the nation is not a happy one. Hope gives way to hate, public health worsens, the divide between rich and poor grows wider, and the rule of law breaks down. Crime increases, as do wars, disease and famine. Refugee and immigration crises spread around the world. And all because we have allowed our vibrations and energies to drop.

When we stop recognising the beauty of the world, the world becomes less beautiful.

With each interaction we have the chance to raise the collective vibration – or not. We can walk past the homeless man in a wide circle, or we can take a minute to speak with him and listen to his story. We can take a moment to check that the old lady who seems to be struggling up the stairs is ok, or we can push past her, annoyed that she's getting in our way. We can hold the door for the person behind us, or we can think solely of our own needs and let it slam in their face.

We can become patrons of our friend's new businesses and choose their products and tell everyone we know. Or we can roll our eyes at their efforts to realise their dream and get our shopping from the supermarket just like we always do. We can give our applause to those who dare to try, or reserve our support for those who are already established in their efforts, lest our own lack of achievement and effort become obvious.

We can turn our backs on those people who need help, those people less fortunate than us, and in doing so contribute to the overall conditions that put them in that situation in the first place.

Everywhere we turn there is an opportunity to be kind. An opportunity to offer encouragement and see from the perspective of the other. Everywhere we turn there is an opportunity to help, or at the very least not be critical and judgemental. And if we can lend a hand up, without expectation of anything in return, and keep doing it and keep doing it, our energy will sing out across the world like a church bell calling everyone to mass.

Be the way you wish the world to be. And one by one, we will make it so.

Let's all adore
In the same well of clouds
This one moon

-    Tagami Kikusha-ni

CHAPTER 15
Love Yourself

"We can always begin again." – **Sharon Salzburg**

Raising our vibration would be a simple exercise if we weren't so addicted to unhappiness and disappointment. We revel in it so much that no matter how much we tell ourselves we want the opposite, we actually find ourselves uncomfortable in the presence of happiness, success and contentment, and view with suspicion and resentment anyone who has found it for themselves.

We take it personally when others succeed or build a happy life for themselves. We see their success as a comment on and a reflection of our failure, and we resent them for it. When we see others come crashing down, we are validated and warmed by the schadenfreude – the good life is a myth, we tell ourselves, and make ourselves comfortable wallowing in our misery.

So attached are we to failure and unhappiness that it has become like an evil twin, steering us away from goodness and reminding us that we are not worthy or deserving of the kind of joy and abundance that we dream of. But if we could somehow draw a line under our failings and simply recognise who we are, and where we are now, in this moment, we would see everything that we have to offer, the wealth that is already ours, and the tools we already possess that we can use to build a better life. We would see success and happiness and joy, and a path to everything we could ever dream of.

But our evil twin is constantly whispering in our ear, urging us to fixate on the past, and worry about the future. It tells us we aren't good enough, that we don't have enough, and we will never be complete unless we have more. It tells us that we will never be happy because we don't deserve to be.

When we fixate on the things – especially the bad things – that have already occurred and which are impossible to change, then we simply relive our failings over and again, until they become a part of our identity. And when we fixate on those things – especially the bad things – that could go wrong in the future, but which haven't even happened yet, we are simply reinforcing an identity of failure upon ourselves. And in each scenario, we are missing the reality of now.

But if we can distract ourselves for a minute, and stop thinking about the past, and stop worrying about the future, we can see ourselves as we really are. We can see our capabilities and limitations without pride and ego getting in the way. We see the healing that we need to undertake, and the improvements that we can make. When we see ourselves in the moment, we see all the skills that we have, the abundant fruits of what we've learned and earned so far, and the wisdom we can share.

When we look at ourselves in this moment, we have a chance to see our beauty and our strengths. Not the misdemeanours and failings of the past, and not the risks or worst-case scenarios of the future. We see our potential. We see what we can achieve. We see how we might achieve it.

We see ourselves.

Only today can we can take action to build upon the foundations of our past, so today is where we must focus our energies. This moment is the only time that anything can occur, and it is up to us to make it happen. And in order to do that we must learn to see ourselves with open eyes, with clarity. We must look beyond the anxiety, beyond the ego and the pride, beyond the traumas of the past and the worries of the future. We must look through our embarrassments, our failings and our weakness, and see who we are, who we can be and what we can do. We must learn to love ourselves unconditionally.

And when we love ourselves it's not an exercise in flattery, but in recognising that we are capable, that we can act with intent to create betterment in our lives, our environment, and the lives of others. We can improve, benefit and build. When we love ourselves it's not an exercise in being proud, but of being confident in who we are, what we can build, and what qualities we can bring. It is about becoming aware of our uniqueness and recognising its assets.

It's about recognising that who we were yesterday doesn't necessarily define who we will be tomorrow.

By being here, in this moment, we can see ourselves – really see ourselves – and start to take the action required to make real our dreams and our goals. By loving ourselves we can release the fear that comes with worrying what other people think of us, as we find our own validation and approval from within. By loving ourselves, we can begin to share our love with the world and everyone in it.

When we love ourselves, we no longer need to defend ourselves as we have the confidence and security to know ourselves. The insinuations of others can offer no threat or intimidation because we know, without doubt, where we lie and who we are. We no longer have anything to fear, and this frees us to act with kindness in everything we do.

By loving ourselves, we can release any perceived threats, because we know that if it doesn't pose a risk of actual physical harm, then there is no danger. The words of others cannot cause us any harm, the only harm is to our pride or ego, and since we have the confidence, self-esteem and assuredness to know ourselves and love ourselves, then our pride and ego cannot be harmed. Any hurt that occurs is simply a result of our own faulty internal processes – of our insecurities and anxieties. When the world causes us pain that is not physical, it is not the world that is at fault but our reaction to it. And as that is an internal reaction – within us and under our control – we can choose to be hurt or not.

We can become invincible.

But this also offers us the opportunity to share our love with the world. As we no longer rely on the people around us for reassurance, validation or permission, and as we are no longer threatened or intimidated or afraid of them for anything other than physical danger, they have no power over us.

It is upon this realisation that we are able to offer love and kindness to even our polar opposites. We can wish love and happiness upon our greatest foes and our fiercest opponents. We can offer loving awareness, loving kindness and the energy of goodwill to those we might otherwise offer hatred and hostility, just as we offer those loving energies to our closest family and friends.

When we love ourselves, we forgive ourselves our past and release the anxieties of the future to appreciate who we are, where we are, and what we have to offer, right here and right now. We can see the humanity in ourselves just as we see it in others, and just as we forgive them and allow them their imperfections, and just as we see their strengths before we see their weakness, we can see our strengths first, too. And we can allow them to grow.

We can tell ourselves that we've punished ourselves enough, and now it's time to get on with the job of recognising our weaknesses and our failings but choosing not to let them define us or become us. When we have separated ourselves from them, we can get on with the important work of being better, of fixing the holes where wind whistles through, of not making the same mistakes again, of being from our past but not of our past, and becoming someone we can be proud of.

And from our central point in the infinite continuum of being, we can nurture a light or integrity, enthusiasm and hope inside us that envelopes us. And when it becomes too bright for us to contain any longer, we can let it shine outwards illuminating even the darkest corners of the universe which we find ourselves at the centre of. And we can let it illuminate others too, who have a world of potential within them.

From this place of love, we can seek to understand ourselves and others, we can seek to acknowledge them, and we can listen – really listen just as we would wish others to listen to us. We can let those who inhabit our universe know that we see them, that we are unjudging and supportive, and that we wish them only joy and wellbeing, just as we would it upon ourselves. We have no adversaries in this existence, only fellow travellers also trying to find their way without a map to guide them.

We can use our light to help others on their way. We can show them the direction that we would wish to take, and give them the space to make their own choices. Love is the most powerful energy in the universe, and there's enough for all of us – it just requires that we share it, and become a beacon that others might navigate by.

As the Buddha taught, a candle can light a thousand more candles and its own light will never be diminished. And so we, too, can help others to burn brightly, but only if our own flame is strong. By looking inwards and releasing all those harmful memories of our past, by silencing those inner voices that would seek to diminish our future, and by trying to be the best, most beautiful versions of ourselves, we can find our flame. And from there we can fan it until it blazes with such ferocity that our warmth is felt around the world.

Our light helps us see ourselves, and it helps us see our world and our purpose in it. And it can also inspire others to do the same. And as our light and the light of others spreads, we will see our energy rippling outwards, like waves on a pond, and our universe will never be the same again.

Here, then, is the meaning of it all – find your light, nourish it, fan its flame until it shines so bright and so hot that it ignites the flames of others, and together we will set the universe alight. And this light will give us meaning beyond the shallow trifles of the materialistic surface world, and we will finally transcend the reality of things that we can touch, taste, buy and consume, and become beings of energy, of creation, and we will build a new reality based on those forgotten ideas of love, hope, and light.

This reality will be different and unique for everyone, each of us at the centre of our own kaleidoscopic universe. But it will be one that encompasses all from which we are hewn, and offer opportunities and hopes beyond anything any of us could have ever imagined before.

Anything is possible. Everything is doable. Just as long as we believe in it and our ability to make it so.

In my hut this spring,
There is nothing –
There is everything!

– Yamaguchi Sodō

Chapter 16
Tend Your Garden

"There are always flowers for those who wish to see them." – Henri Matisse

A garden left untended grows weeds and pests. Parasites eat the rose bushes, and the grasses rise dense and impenetrable. Wild animals roam freely, causing havoc among the abandoned ornaments, while magpies disturb the peace with their acerbic calls and aggression. Where once a fountain brought a vibrant pond to life with graceful goldfish performing slow-motion underwater acrobatics, now the water is stagnant, and mosquito larva grow undisturbed beneath the thick duckweed, ready to launch themselves skyward to feast on the blood of any unsuspecting passers-by.

This was once a taste of paradise, but the gardener became distracted from his duties and, having not pulled out the weeds or pruned the bushes for years now, can only look on at this overgrown mess of abandonment with shame and disparity. His joints now too stiff to tackle the problem. His back aches too much to bend down and pull up the weeds, his knees too sore to rake or dig.

An untended garden left to its own devices always becomes wild and unforgiving. Impenetrable, its vines become entangled, its paths overgrown, no room to take shelter under the branches of its trees, the sunlight struggling to break through the knots and tangles of brush and bramble.

A tended garden, however, remains young and vibrant, along with its gardener. Blackbirds sing from the trees, whose fruit are collected for pies and desserts, and goldfish dance gleefully beneath the crystal waters, feeding on the passing insects that rest on the surface, and entertaining the gardener, should he pause from his duties trimming the lawns, cutting the hedges and harvesting the fragrant flowers as a gift for his loved one.

It's peaceful here – a haven from the noise and chaos of the outside world. Only the sounds of the water and the dull thud of the shishi-odoshi distracting from the gentle birdsong and the buzz of the bees who move from flower to flower collecting nectar to make their honey.

This is a place to escape to, a place that revitalises those who wish to find solitude here. But that peace comes at a price. Leaves must be raked, borders tidied, dead heads removed, and weeds plucked from the soil. This work alone is enough to keep the gardener young and supple, and the rewards of calm refuge from unwanted distractions are worth the minor toil to keep the plants in order and the pathways clear.

The tended garden is a place where the air is fresh, and each breath fills the lungs with energy, purging them of their doubt. As well as the roses, the hostas, the apple trees and the acers, other things grow here too. Hope takes root in the shade of the orchard, ideas spring up among the Japanese ornaments, and grace, equanimity and tranquillity beg to be picked and savoured as they grow entwined among the strawberries. Happiness grows tall like the sunflowers, and contentment spreads throughout the greenery, planting itself in every corner it can find. This is heaven. Here right now. In the well-tended garden.

Among the weeds and tendrils that grow unabated in the untended garden, though, are found plants of a different nature. In the dank, heavy soil beneath the thick grasses sprout the dark spiny fronds of anxiety and fear. Paranoia and disempowerment grow like creepers around the stems of an old rosemary bush, strangling the life out of it until its delicate fragrance has long departed on the passing wind. Biting insects suck away confidence and self-esteem, leaving behind itches that lead to hostility, conflict and hatred. Bitterness and resentment permeate the air like the smells of rot and mould.

Everywhere, thorny stems force their way through the tangle of dead branches and knotty, gnarly roots, prickling anyone who attempts to find their way through the wilderness. It seems impossible that this was once a neat and tidy paradise, with so much to offer. Yet beneath the thorns, and the wasp nests, and the tangle of roots, that paradise still persists.

If the gardener who left this former paradise untended could remember the time before, if he could believe that beneath all of this wretched and rotten overgrowth there is an Eden waiting to be set free, he might, just once, pick up his sheers and cut back a single bramble to peer at what lies beneath.

And doing so he would feel his joints becoming looser and less sore, and find himself energised to cut back some more. With each click of his sheers his muscles ease and grow stronger, the aches subside, and his efforts become easier and less taxing.

With just a little effort each day, paradise begins to reveal itself once more. And as the grasses give way to lawns, and the gardener's joints grow supple and his muscle are made strong by the small efforts of tidying, digging, pruning and planting, paradise is regained. And as he watches the goldfish dancing under the fountain the old gardener catches his reflection in the crystal waters of the now reborn pond, and sees himself as a young man.

Reclining beneath the apple tree to survey his good work he breathes deeply. Why had it taken so long to find this oasis of peace beneath the chaos of the untended weeds? Why had he allowed them to take over this space that offers so much respite and revitalisation? Would he ever allow the weeds to take hold again?

The wise gardener understands that creating such a beautiful Eden is a daily practice. Plant flowers, pull up the weeds and enjoy the benefits of your labours as you walk among the lush beds, your feet cushioned on the soft chamomile lawns. But turn your back and before long the roses succumb to the pests, the weeds strangle the flowers, and you grow all the things that make a garden a hostile and unwelcoming place. Where will you go to rest when the creepers become too wild?

Better to nurture your paradise, and create your own haven for rest and repair, and remain young and happy in the process.

There is nothing you can
See that is not a flower;
There is nothing you can
Think that is not the moon.

   – Matsuo Bashō

Chapter 17
STOP

"What is this life if, full of care,
We have no time to stand and stare."
– William Henry Davies

Wherever you are, stop. Whatever you're doing, just stop. Put down what you're holding. Stop walking, driving, talking. That thought in your head that's overwhelming you right now, just stop.

Put down your phone. Turn off the television. Step away from your computer.

Stop.

In any given moment, we are multidimensional beings. While we exist in this plain of reality, we are usually in another at the same time. Sometimes more than one. Yes, we might be walking down the street, but we are also looking at our phone, absorbed into the Internet, or email, or text messages.

We might be sat on the train, but we're also in the world of the book we're reading, absorbed in the escapist fantasy of the other world we're lost in.

We might be sitting on the sofa, next to our loved ones, and at the same time focused on the soap opera that's on the television. We might be sat in the cinema, but we're absorbed into the movie we're watching.

We might be having a conversation, but really we're thinking about how we'll find the money to pay the bills this month. Or what are we going to say to our parents when they find out about the thing. Or the leaking pipe in the kitchen. Or the strange man who was sat in his car on your road when you left for work this morning. Or whether or not to buy that jacket you've had your eye on.

But right now, in this moment, you need to pull yourself back from whichever other dimensions you are inhabiting, and just inhabit this one.

Just stop.

Where are you now. Are you standing? Sitting? Leaning against the wall? Is it warm or cold? What are you wearing? Are your shoes too tight? Is your t-shirt loose, or your sweatshirt warm and cosy? What does the fabric feel like against your skin? Is it soft or coarse?

What is the light like where you are right now? Is it a bright sunny day, or are you sat in a dark room with low lighting? Are there people here? Are they talking? What other sounds can you hear?

Maybe it's quiet and all you can hear is the sound of your own breathing, and the vague hum of the electric devices in the room. Maybe somewhere, in a nearby apartment or a passing car, music is playing. Can you make it out, or is it too far away? Is that a plane in the distance, or a police siren a few streets away?

Move your fingers. Just one to begin with. And then two. Keep going until all your fingers are moving, wiggling. How does it feel? Can you feel the air moving around them? Now move your toes, and then your feet. How does it feel when you breathe in, and then breathe out? Can you feel the air moving down your trachea into your chest? Does it feel cool and fresh? Can you feel your chest rising and falling?

What are you in contact with right now? Are you sitting? Leaning? Standing? Whatever you're in contact with, if it's a wall, or a floor, or the bed, or a chair, what does it feel like pressed against you? Can you feel the texture of the fabric? Is it warm? Is it soft or hard?

If you're standing on a train or a bus, what does the handrail feel like? Is it cold metal, or warm plastic? Does it make you feel safe, like you won't fall over if there is a sudden jolt?

Now look up. What do you see? Is it just the ceiling? What colours are there, how smooth is it? Are there ceiling panels, or just a smooth flat surface? What kind of lighting is there? How bright is it?

If you're outdoors, what does the sky look like? Is it a grey, cloudy day, or is it a clear blue sky? Are there any little fluffy clouds? What do they look like? Is there a breeze blowing? How does it feel against your skin? Perhaps there's rain in the air. Is its heavy rain, light

191

drizzle, or just the occasional fat drop? Is it cold? Warm? Is it soaking you through or barely noticeable?

How does your body feel? Are you shivering in the cold, or are you comfortably warm? Perhaps you prefer things to be on the cooler side? Are you hungry or are you full? Are you tired? What does the skin on your arms feel like? Do you have any itches? Any aches or pains?

Now close your eyes. What do you see? Is it pitch black, or is the bright sunlight seeping through your eyelids? Or do you see throbbing colours and patterns, moving and changing? What shapes do you see? Can you focus on them long enough to get a good view of them, or do they always avoid your concentrated gaze?

Now, with your eyes shut, listen again to the noises around you. Can you hear cars passing by on the streets outside? As they swish past on the road outside, can you imagine that the sounds they make are not vehicle sounds but the sounds of waves crashing against the shore? Can you picture yourself on the beach, feeling the sand under your feet, and the sun on your face, soaking up the atmosphere of a tropical escape?

If there's no traffic nearby, but just the noise of people talking, can you picture yourself surrounded by a vast expanse of birds – a sea of pink flamingos, chattering away, all standing on one leg with you among them?

If you're alone apart from the sound of your breathing and the vague buzz of your electricals, can you picture yourself floating in the darkness of space, in your spacesuit, just the sound of your breath and your life support systems for company as you drift into the warm arms of infinity?

Where are you now? How does it sound? Where can it take you? Where could you be in this moment if you were to open the portal of your mind and allow yourself to be transported away? Which dimension would you be in? Would you even be you?

What would it feel like to have the alpine wind beneath your wings, or the feeling of the ocean against your scales, or the arctic snow against your fur?

Or would you rather be here, right now, experiencing these sounds, feeling, smells, light or darkness as they really are? Really focusing on what your body is experiencing in this very moment. The joy of textures, the spectrum of smells and temperatures. The sensation of movement, the feeling of your limbs as they move, and as the world moves around them.

At any given moment, we have the freedom to be anywhere, do anything, be anyone or anything. We can choose to fixate and ruminate on the things that aren't working for us in the shallow surface world, or we can lose ourselves in any of the infinite other dimensions that are available to us if we should just choose to step into them. We can disappear into music, escape into art, imagine kaleidoscopic galaxies.

Or we can be here now. Lose ourselves in the present, in this very moment. We can choose to give our energy to honouring, celebrating and respecting the now. This reality of experience, sensation, sound, taste, smell and touch is available to us whenever we need it. All we have to do is stop.

To own our reality we simply need to decide what to focus on, and to focus with intent. Decide not to drift, not to be distracted, but to focus on a feeling, or an idea, or a picture, or a sound. Focus all our attention on a thing of our choosing. To really experience, for ourselves, the power of awareness.

And when we are aware of the thing that we're focused on – that sense of touch, the feeling of our feet in our shoes, the sound of our breath within our space suit, the imaginary sand beneath our toes, step back – and stop once again. Observe your awareness.

Observe yourself focused on your breathing. Observer yourself transforming the sounds of traffic into waves crashing on the beach. Observe yourself lost in the sensation of the movement of your fingers and toes. And become aware of your awareness.

Where are you now? As you watch yourself two-steps abstracted, who is doing the watching, and who is being watched? Are you a body with a soul, or a soul with a body? Where does one begin and the other end? Are you the person named on your birth certificate, or are you infinite layers of awareness, each observing the other in an ever-expanding spiral of consciousness?

Are you the person named on your bank statement, or are you part of an infinite continuum of being? Where do you end and where does your consciousness begin?

Karl Jung wrote "beneath the threshold of consciousness everything was seething with life" and to appreciate this all we have to do is stop, extract ourselves from our awareness and be its witness. When we transcend the two-dimensional reality of the surface world, an infinite spectrum of possibility opens up to us. No restrictions, no limits, just freedom to know that anything that can be imagined can be real.

We were born with a universe at our fingertips – unlimited souls launched into a world of unlimited possibilities. As we grew up we fell into a framework of values dictated by society. But these restrictions serve only the system, and while they enable us to function within it, they are only real because we make them real. We only stop at a red light because we agree on its value.

But when we reach beyond this framework and stretch our wings, there are no limits. Not even the reality of physics and the laws of science can prevent us exploring multiple dimensions of being – as long as we free our minds enough to go beyond what we have been taught is real.

We are at the centre of our universe, and it stretches out in every direction, backwards in time, forwards into the future, and we are connected to every possibility by infinite ethereal threads. Even the impossible, once imagined, becomes possible.

So where are you now? Right this minute? Where can you go? What can you feel? Who can you be? Because everything is available to you. You just have to accept your ultimate freedom.

Sitting quietly, doing
Nothing, Spring comes, and
The grass grows, by itself.

- Matsuo Bashō

CHAPTER 18
START

"The best way to start doing something is to start doing something." – Vernon Howard

There is a decisive moment, a fundamental point in the existence of everything, where the collective energies of momentum, inertia and intent reach such a critical mass that something happens. And until that moment, it doesn't.

Nothing happens, until something happens.

This instance – this flashpoint – is something that has occurred for everything along the continuum of being. It is the intersection where before and after collide, and the appropriate energies give birth to something new. It is, for everything and anything, the start.

The start, or beginning, or birth, is a vital and intrinsic part of the existence of anything. Everything has to start somewhere, at some point or some moment, and until it does, it cannot be. It is that simple. The start of anything is just as important – and perhaps infinitely more so – than any other moment in its lifecycle or beyond. Without a start nothing can be.

Yet as soon as something has begun its fate is sealed and its very existence ripples backwards in time along the continuum of being – now that it has come into being, it was always destined to be and was so with such certainty that it was as good as real before it even began. Just as the oak exists in the acorn, once something begins it was always real — only in an abstract, non-tangible way.

As sentient beings we struggle with the notion of being. Uncomfortable in our own skin, we struggle to understand why we're here, what's the point or what does it all mean. But really, all we need to know and find peace in is the notion that we began at a particular moment in time, and that enables us – empowers us – to simply be.

What could be purer and more authentic that just being? Just acknowledging our existence and finding the time and the space to simply be here, now, in this moment, as our start prescribed. This is what we strive for in meditation, in the exploration of meaning and the purpose of our existence, and the sense of simply being is perhaps the ultimate answer to any existential crisis.

Only, we demand more than that.

And the notion of the start gives us something to hang our hats on. Before the start it wasn't, and after the start it is – and always has been. What more could we need or want? All our questions answered, all conundrums deemed mute in the simplification of the entire purpose of humanity. Simply, to be.

Alongside love and kindness, the act of starting must be one of the most powerful forces in the universe and beyond. The universe had its start in the Big Bang. The planet earth had its start as dust spinning around our primordial flaming sun began to clump together in bigger lumps. Life on this planet had its start when lightning produced just the right conditions for genetic material to be produced, catalysing the surrounding chemicals into a self-sustaining process of replication.

Everything must have a start somewhere, and in any given moment we find ourselves at the start of the next. Every second of every day we have the opportunity to start something new, something that, if we didn't start it right now, would never happen. We have the chance to be reborn, the chance to create something unique, the chance of a fresh beginning where just seconds ago there was nothing at all.

We are surrounded by fresh starts, we are the product of them, and everything we are enjoying, suffering from, or benefitting from began somewhere. Many of these starts were beyond our control, yet we have immense power over others. At all moments in our existence, we have the opportunity to bring something into being, simply by choosing to start.

We initiate dreams in our head that we couldn't enjoy unless they had a start. But we can also make them real, here in the surface world if we are prepared to give them the start they need. If we start now we can climb mountains, feed the poor, bring music to the ears of millions, and cure all of mankind's ills. But only if we start now.

If we start now, we can set in motion a chain of events that will alter our reality beyond recognition. This time next year we could be free of debts, we could be slimmer, fitter, more accomplished, more educated. If we start now we have the opportunity to craft a reality so wonderful we'll sing our own praises from the highest vantage point this time next year. Or in ten years. Or in twenty years.

If we start now we can build something that we'll look back upon with great pride.

If we start now we can change the patterns that became part of us a long time ago, which have held us back, caused us pain, or got us this far but no further. If we start now, we can build a tomorrow that exceeds our wildest dreams, and we can build a version of ourselves that will look back at us with such gratitude we will wish we'd started sooner.

In the entirety of history, all great things have been brought into being by starting. It doesn't matter where they started, or how they started, just that they started. This is how the pyramids of Giza were built, how man walked on the moon, how Da Vinci painted the Mona Lisa, and how Velcro was created. With a start.

Sometimes the thing that started becomes a huge empire, and rains wealth upon the person of who started it. Sometimes the thing that's started never gets any further at all. Indeed, along the road of achievement the gutters are littered with ideas that started but went nowhere.

Yet, similarly, just past the finish line is an infinite number of ideas – some very good, some very bad –

that are blessed with being started. If they weren't to be, it would be a very different picture indeed. But whether they fail or whether they succeed, the one thing that all activities have in common is that they started. If we walk in the forest, we find ourselves surrounded by seeds that started the germination process to become trees. In the shallow surface world we find ourselves surrounded by material things which all, at one point or another, started on the drawing board of the designer. In the arms of our loved ones we find ourselves in a blessed position that would seem alien to us had the relationship we are lucky enough to find ourselves in not started.

Starting, it seems, is the vital element to the existence of everything. But when was the last time we created something afresh, started something new? When did we last harness the power of starting to enjoy life, to craft our existence, or to build something? When did we last start something that we'll thank ourselves for in a decade?

It doesn't require a clap of thunder to start something amazing. Nor does it require divine intervention. All that you need in order to start something – anything – is the intent to make it happen, the will to create the appropriate action, and the belief that from this start something will come into being that didn't exist before.

What will you start today that could send your life in a different direction? What could you start to bring benefits where previously there were none? What could you start to challenge your existing status quo? What could you start to aid those less fortunate than yourself? What small thing could you start today that will grow to something gargantuan over a year, or two, or ten?

How can you start shaping the rest of your life today?

The tree cut,
Dawn breaks early
At my little window.

— Masaoka Shiki

CHAPTER 19
Let Go

"When I let go of what I am, I become what I might be." – Lao Tzu

As long as anything can trigger a reaction within us, we are not our own masters. When we feel outraged by a news story, upset by a bully, angered by a colleague, or enticed by the notion of something new, we are in the grip of an external force that has a power over us. And that grip is a direct reflection of an attachment of our own.

The more we hold on to something, the more of a hold it has on us. Everything is a reflection of our inner state.

When we feel anger, sadness or even happiness, we must recognise that these states are not caused by the person, or the thing, or the incident that we're having feelings about, but they are instead an internal process. We feel emotions internally, they are created within us, yet we allow them to be triggered by external stimuli. And until we understand that we are the gatekeeper and until now we've left the door wide open to anyone or anything that wishes to walk in with their muddy boots and trample all over our emotions, then we will forever be at the mercy of external forces. And the stronger those forces will become.

The bully feeds off our reactions, and finds themselves empowered to bully us even more. But if we were to refuse to allow them to trigger emotions within us, we would take away their power altogether by simply not reacting, and they would lose interest. The best advertisements connect with us on an emotional level, and we allow them to trigger a response within us that leads to the actions that the advertiser wishes us to undertake.

Our emotions are not caused by the external stimulus, but they are triggered by our own sensitivities. If this weren't true would all be angered by the same things, amused by the same things, outraged, offended and hurt by the same things.

When we reach a level of awareness that takes responsibility for our own internal processes rather than blaming external stimuli, then we have reached a position of insight that will, with practice, enable us to do one of the most powerful things possible. That is, to let go.

When we learn the intrinsic power of letting go, of the release of tension that has previously caused us to be triggered by various stimuli, we can begin to practice owning our internal processes. We can begin recognising the things that cause us harm, that have power over us, and take steps to break free of the illusion that external influences are responsible for our internal state.

And, paradoxically, we can then start the practice of nurturing an internal state that not only serves us better, but which begins to influence the outside world.